DENT

DENT

THE HIGHEST MAINLINE STATION IN ENGLAND

W R MITCHELL

FOREWORD BY MICHAEL OWEN
(Chairman, Friends of the Settle-Carlisle Line)

...we raced across two massive viaducts
in quick succession, Dent Head and
Arten Gill...Then the line starts scoring
points, dealing only in superlatives.

Alexander Frater, in *The Observer* (1983).

CASTLEBERG
1995

For
CHARLIE EMETT
a long-time devotee of the Settle-Carlisle

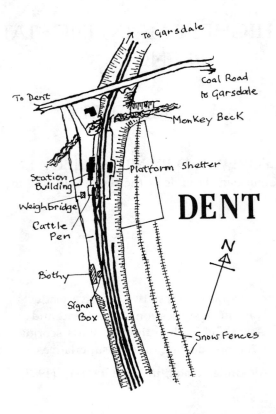

A **Castleberg** Book.

First published in the United Kingdom in 1995.

Copyright © W R Mitchell 1995.

The moral right of the author has been asserted.

ISBN 1 871064 93 7

Typeset in Palacio, printed and bound in the United Kingdom by
Lamberts Printers, Station Road, Settle, North Yorkshire, BD24 9AA.

Published by Castleberg, 18 Yealand Avenue, Giggleswick, Settle,
North Yorkshire, BD24 0AY.

Contents

Introduction   9

First Impressions   12

Dalesfolk and Engineers   17

The Railway Cometh   22

Steam on the Drag   37

Where Shall We Put the Station?   41

Thirsty Expresses   45

Coal, Cattle and Coffins   47

The Stationmasters   56

Stationmaster's House   61

Permanent Way   68

In the Signal Box   72

The White Stuff   80

Garsdale Troughs   91

The Tunnel Gang   94

Social Life   100

The War Years   102

Brave New World   114

AN "OLD DERBY 4" LEAVES
THE SOUTH PORTAL OF
RISE HILL TUNNEL

Illustrations

Jenny Holmes — 8, 19, 25, 54-5, 63
Peter Fox — 1, 4, 6, 11, 16, 30, 43, 44, 53, 60, 67, 74, 76,
        79, 84, 86, 91, 93, 101, 103, 106, 121
Richard Bancroft — 2, 99
F S Williams, *The Midland Railway* — 22, 36
British Rail — 118

Foreword

by Michael Owen
(Chairman, Friends of the Settle-Carlisle Line)

HAVING just emerged from Bleamoor Tunnel portal, one is confronted with what I think is one of the most beautiful and breathtaking three miles of railway in the United Kingdom. Running parallel on a ledge above the infant Yorkshire River Dee, passengers have the opportunity to discern the idyllic beauty of Dentdale.

In the distance, looming towards the train is the highest railway station in England—Dent, surrounded by creaking snow fences and once protected by a Midland Railway style signal box which is with us no more.

In order to reach Dent station during this brief encounter with Dentdale, the train crosses two of the most photographed viaducts on the Settle-Carlisle Railway. Not only are they the highest but the most striking and magnificent structures, epitomising the Victorian value of doing things properly on a grandiose scale.

The story of Dent, on the Settle-Carlisle, has been compiled by Bill Mitchell in a most readable way, much of it based on interviews with local people. I wish the book every success.

The Stationmaster's House was made on a plan used throughout the Settle-Carlisle system, though the building materials varied, some houses being built of brick, some of limestone and some of New Red Sandstone.

Dent was exceptional in having double-windows and also walls clad with slate to deflect the weather at 1,150 ft.

Generally, Stationmasters were provided with accommodation which included a large kitchen, living room and lounge. Three bedrooms were available, but there was no bathroom, such a domestic feature being quite rare in the 1890s.

There was a washhouse and outside privvy at the back. To reach them, the Stationmaster and his family crossed a wind-swept yard.

Introduction

A BOOK about Dent station? What is there to know, apart from the fact that it is the highest mainline station in England? And that it has barriers of up-ended railway sleepers to keep snow off the tracks? The Stationmaster's House was provided with double-glazed windows and at Dent a stone cabin was used as a haven for exhausted snow-clearers. A visit to Dent station is a thrilling experience when a Steam Special is storming the Drag—those first 20 miles of the Settle-Carlisle where the ruling gradient is 1 in 100.

The elevation of the platforms given on a sign by the up-platform at Dent is 1,150 feet, but the figure varies according to which book you are reading. Jenny Holmes, who lives at the former Stationmaster's House, read that the platforms are 1,139 feet and that her home is on the 1,150 feet contour. The fences which were made of redundant sleepers proved to be of little value when snow arrived on a North-East wind which is full of spite. The space between two of them was used as a Home Guard firing range during the 1939-45 war.

The windows of the Stationmaster's House were not double-glazed in the modern sense of two panes being set slightly apart in the same frame. The Midland architect arranged to cheat the wind by setting two windows six inches apart. Cecil Sanderson, a former Stationmaster, had a novel way of sealing the House against draughts in the worst of the winter. He sprayed the house with water from a hosepipe, forming a protective shield of ice. Incidentally, the snow-clearers had a special name for their stone-clad refuge near the signal box. They called it The Dent Hotel.

My fascination with the Settle-Carlisle began with tales told by my godfather, Ted Boak, one of the drivers on the Drag. Then I read Houghton's and Foster's account, in prose and picture, published in 1948 under the title *The Story of the Settle-Carlisle Line*. The style as well as the content impressed me. Chapter One begins: "There is a railway line in England which fights its way over the gaunt Pennine uplands to make a vital communication between South and North. A line which tested to the utmost the peerless constructional skill of British railway engineers. A line which braves the rugged contours of wild fell and striding dale, and which defies the freakish, unpredictable weather of its chosen path...The name of this stretch of railroad steel—seventy-three miles of it—is the Settle-Carlisle line."

I have been collecting information about Dent station for forty years. Jack Sedgwick, the last of the Dent signalmen, allowed me to make notes from items in his collection, including a register of deliveries to Dent at the turn of the century. Roy and Jenny Holmes have given me some lively contemporary stories. Isabel Raw, a farmer's wife at Cow Dub, recalled for me the effort needed to visit her mother when she had young children and a pram to push. She first climbed the 600 feet of winding road from Lea Yeat to Dent Station and then travelled by train to Garsdale, changing for Hawes. Here she had a mile and a-half walk to her mother's home. A few hours later, she had to think about the return journey.

I have been lucky to draw on the memories of footplate men, who thrashed the old steamers up the Drag. A Skipton man, on his first trip as fireman, was almost blown off the footplate at Dent Head Viaduct. He managed to grasp a handle and hold on. This man was "firing" a Compound. He spoke of the difficulty of throwing coal through a narrow hole into an eleven foot firebox, and placing each shovelful precisely, as the wind roared about the cab.

The stimulus to write a book about Dent station came after I had met Cecil Sanderson—nicknamed Sandy—who was Stationmaster here from 1938 until 1945. As far as I know, it is the first book to deal with this subject. The general style of this book is gossipy. If, in the old days, a Settle-Carlisle man was asked about the source of a tit-bit of information, and if he did not want to disclose it, he would say: ''Old Meg told me''. If someone asked about a matter on which the railwayman was ignorant, he might reply: ''Old Meg'll knaw!'' Over the years, Meg has become a real person to railwaymen working between Appleby and Dent. She is everyone's favourite aunt, wise and discreet in turn.

It has been a joy to record tales about Dent which have come from the lips of those who experienced them.

ARTEN GILL

First Impressions

In April, 1877, the Rev D Adams, Vicar of Cowgill, wrote to the Midland suggesting that the new station to be opened at Dent should be known simply by that name. To this the company not unnaturally agreed.

Peter E Baughan, 1966.

On a clear spring day, the two and a-half miles from Blea Moor to Dent station are incomparably the finest of the whole line, with stunning glimpses down Dentdale as the train swings out of cuttings and across viaducts.

Derek Cross, in centenary year, 1976.

WHEN the Settle-Carlisle celebrated its centenary in 1976, I asked Eric Treacy, the "Railway Bishop", for his favourite memory. He recalled being on the footplate of a clean rebuilt Scot, driven by Wee George Dransfield, a Holbeck man. "Up the bank, beautifully crisp 3-cylinder beat, exhaust shooting up into the sky. Air as fresh as you only get in Ribblesdale; sky bright blue with white fluffy clouds. The hills purple and friendly. Blea Moor tunnel, dark and damp. Then, a moment of unforgettable splendour, as the train burst out of the tunnel and there, to the west, Dentdale presents itself as a place of peaceful beauty, tempting the traveller to pull the communication cord and get off the train to stay in this 'Shangri-la'."

Arthur Raistrick, the Dales historian, wrote enthusiastically about the glimpse of Dentdale from a northbound train. "The line emerges high on the side of steep fells, with a breathtaking view over the head of Dentdale across to the mass of Whernside. Two more impressive viaducts cross gorge-like torrent courses, and then the train roars through Dent station, the highest on the line...with a massive range of snow fences along the fell side above it."

O S Nock, railway historian, who was affectionately known as Ozzie, provided me with his favourite memory of a line he had known since boyhood at Giggleswick School. He also opted for a footplate experience to the north of Blea Moor. Ozzie had the exhilaration of crossing Dent Head viaduct and travelling through Rise Hill Tunnel, "out again on to that dizzy ledge above Garsdale to the highest water troughs in England." The driver, lowering his scoop at 60 m.p.h., had misjudged the amount of water in hand. In seconds, the tank had overflowed. "Involuntarily, I ducked, for the water came over in a solid cascade and hit our cab glasses with a roar rather than a splash."

Arthur Raistrick, who was not normally one to eugolise, must be allowed a second appraisal. He recalled that, at the approach to Dent, a traveller has for a few minutes the sensation of suspension a matter of hundreds of feet above a half-real scene. As the train plunged into the next tunnel, the passenger was left with a sense of having looked for an instant through "some magic door to see a bit of an unreal world."

The Settle-Carlisle, beloved by thousands, was the railway which no one really wanted. The young and thrustful Midland Company, rebuffed when it approached the London and North-Western for better facilities on the Lancaster-Carlisle route, in order to improve its trade with Scotland, decided to make its own costly way to Carlisle. When the LNWR realised the Midland meant business, it relented, but Parliament—having seen so many grand railway ideas cancelled—insisted that the work should proceed. The Midland shrugged its shoulders, totted up its cash reserves, asked the best engineer, John Crossley, to supervise the work (despite his impending retirement, which he delayed) and built a superbly-engineered, all-weather route—a railway in the clouds.

The surveyors took advantage of two north-south valleys, the Ribble and the Eden, and crossed the High Fell country with a dizzying succession of major works—14 tunnels, 21 viaducts and no less than 325 bridges. The construction work took place in frightful weather, with a higher-than-average rainfall, winds strong and cold enough to put ice crystals in the bloodstream, days of low cloud and also a minor earthquake! The Midland board budgetted the cost of their new railway at £2,200,000 and (in February, 1876) were told that the total cost was expected to be £3,467,000—or £47,500 a mile.

Even today, the Settle-Carlisle summer is but a blink between two long winters. For every day when Dentdale is revealed with clarity and colour, there are several days when clouds drape the fells like wet dish-cloths. The Helm Wind, brewed up around High Cup Nick, on the East Fellside, rampages as far as Garsdale and Dent. It had a reputation for blowing cobs of coal off the shovels of firemen working on the exposed footplates of early locomotives. In the deep midwinter, the tunnels are draped with icicles which might weigh up to two tons and be as thick as a man's body.

On Centenary Day, in 1976, when it was theoretically springtime, our special train arrived at a cold, windswept Dent station to find a reception party which included a hospital consultant and his wife (dressed as a navvy and his missus) and two local ladies (in old-time clothes and knitting in the old Dent style as they talked). Helpers who were also dressed-up offered the chilled passengers some ice cream. There were profuse thanks—but few takers.

The Midland assault on the High Fells transformed the life of what had been a tract of secluded dale country, with a few scattered farms connected to the villages by roads which had an aversion to going straight. Blea Moor was simply a wild tract crossed by the Lancaster-Richmond turnpike and frequented by Lile Hob, a mischievous wee creature who waited for travellers and then rode on the back of horse or cart.

Clearly, the coming of the Iron Hose did not appeal to him. He was not seen from the day a traction engine and caravan brought the first engineers and their men to Ribblehead in 1869.

Blea Moor became famous for its echoing tunnel and the fact that telegraph wires across the moor had corks fitted to them so they would be seen by local red grouse in their headlong dash to escape shooters. If the tunnel had a super-natural presence, it would surely be the ghost of some careless miner who died when using dynamite. Or a nineteen-shillings-a-week lengthman, struck by a train when moving in the smoky gloom, tapping a stick against a rail to keep on the right course.

With Blea Moor to the south and Rise Hill to the north, the Dent stretch of the Settle-Carlisle has a tunnel on either end. Willie Davison, a permanent way man and Methodist local preacher, who lived in one of the cottages near the south por-tal of Blea Moor Tunnel, told me of the unusual route he followed if he had a preaching appointment in Dent. He pushed his bicycle through Blea Moor and beside the track until he reached the road at Dent Head, whereupon he could free-wheel most of the way down the dale to Dent Town. After the service, he had a similar (but much more strenuous) journey home. He told me of the local preacher who, cycling into a headwind, prayed that the direction of the wind might change. It did. He had a headwind for the return trip.

The Settle-Carlisle, tucked away on its fellside ledge, has always seemed curiously detached from life in Dentdale. One frosty night, while visiting a farmstead, I heard the sound of an approaching train and looked across the dale, and high up, to where it was passing with a glare from the locomotive and a light in every window. It resembled some fiery dragon breathing sparks. Four and a-half winding, twisting miles separate Dent Town from Dent station. The 600 feet climb to the station inhibits the pedestrian. In the old days, it warmed up the horses of the carriers. Matthew Howarth, a coal agent, drove a motor bike to and from his work at the station. He was also the newspaper chap, tucking some 'papers into his belt and stacking others on the petrol tank of his machine. He threw off papers at the various homes.

Queen Elizabeth slept at Dent station, breaking a journey to Appleby, the county town of Old Westmorland. She was spared the discomfort of the waiting room. The Royal Train was parked in the siding. A train carrying the Queen Mother had an overnight stop at Dent and there were the customary checks by police and others of bridges and tunnels to ensure that all was well before her southward journey was resumed. Down at Ribblehead, not long before the Royal Train was due, panic developed as ganger and lengthmen rounded up cows which had broken out of pens at the cattle dock and wandered off towards Selside.

Dalesfolk and Engineers

There is a town of little note or praise,
Narrow and winding are its rattling streets,
Where cart with cart in cumbrous conflict meets.

Samuel Taylor Coleridge.

DENTDALE was for centuries a Yorkshire valley, being part of the old West Riding. A good sixty miles, as the crow flies, separated Dent from Wakefield, the county town. Dent Town and Sedbergh were on a finger of land stretching out from Yorkshire to tickle the ribs of Westmorland. At the local government reorganisation of 1974, Westmorland was eliminated and the new county of Cumbria scooped up Dentdale. The pen proved to be mightier than the sword!

In truth, there had been a strong flavour of Westmorland in Dentdale. It was reflected in the dialect, in the custom of whitening the faces of farmhouses and in the view down the valley of Howgill Fells, the "naked heights" of Wordsworth, smooth and dome-shaped as compared with the bare sheep ridges and moors of the Yorkshire Dales, though Dent was to continue to be part of the Dales National Park. Kendal, a town built on the woollen trade, sent wool to Dent to sustain the activity of the local hand-knitters, who turned out gloves, mittens, bonnets and stockings. These were collected when the next load of wool arrived in the village.

Dentdale is divided into four distinctive areas. Working from top to bottom, they are Deepdale (locally pronounced Dipt'l), Cowgill (which has its own church), Dent Town and Gawthrop. The valley begins at Stot Scales, near where the Midland Railway Company constructed their Dent Head

17

viaduct, and runs out at Peggleside Farm, about a mile from, Sedbergh. Dent Town, the only place of any size in a dale noted for its numerous farmsteads, is brooded over by a church founded in Norman times.

The villagers have a fierce sense of pride, dating from the time when their town was more important than Sedbergh, whose voters used to trudge to Dent at election times until the year 1863. The motto of Dentalians might well be: "Who dares to meddle with us?" Their favourite son, Adam Sedgwick, was a pioneer geologist with a face as craggy as the rocks he studied. His memorial is an upreared slab of granite in the cobbled main street, where the teeth of motorists chatter like castanets and a woman wearing high heels winces at every footfall.

Dent Town has a cosy, valley botton situation. Within a few miles, the road, having traversed a narrow, steep-sided valley, is losing itself on the moors. Fells soar to clear the 1,200 feet contour line and cluster around the dalehead, which consequently retains the winter frost-chill until well into the official springtime. Isolated Dentdale developed a character of its own. You may have heard the old saying: "Do as they do in Dent—if you have no baccy, chew bent [a type of hill grass]."

When the Settle-Carlisle was proposed, there was little real wealth in Dentdale. At the middle of the century, there had been steady work for skilled men in the enclosure of the commons with drystone walls. There were jobs in farming, in quarrying, at the marble works and (a few) in the coal pits. In "railway time", when some of the dalesfolk provided lodgings for workmen, they marvelled at the primitive conditions of some of the lodgings. The water supply to some cottages was augmented by "soft water" [rain], collected in tubs and ice formed on the water-tub in winter. Sometimes it was necessary to break the ice using a hammer. One (and possibly more than one) of the dale toilets, found at the bottom of the garden, had three holes on the seat. The holes

18

DENTDALE FROM ABOVE THE
STATIONMASTER'S HOUSE

were respectively large, medium and small.

The weather of Dentdale "suits itself" and "wean't let itsel
be bossed by t'weather forecasters". In winter, the road in
the lower part of the dale is wet. Further up the valley, it is
icebound. In a nutshell, it's a top-coat colder at Cowgill.
Living at Dent station, Jenny Holmes remarks that she
sometimes needs three thousand jumpers. The station lies

just off Galloway Gate (popularly called the Coal Road), an ancient track, now tarmacadamed, which served the coal pits at Cowgill Head, rose to 1,761 feet at Shaking Moss, and then ran near the pits on the Garsdale side. Minor tracks lead to a scattering of other pits, all relatively shallow, extending to the seven or eight inch seams of hard, brittle coal which formed part of the Yoredale Series of rocks. The trade fell away when the Settle-Carlisle ensured a good supply of deep-mined coal from South Yorkshire.

Old Adam (Sedgwick) left us vivid word pictures of t'auld life i' Dentdale and mentioned the coal pits. A dalesman had recounted that when he began work as a miner at the age of nine, he provided his own candles and knee-pads. Laden tubs were drawn out by men who moved on hands and knees. During winter, the only daylight seen by these human moles was on Sundays. Trains of packhorses were used to transport the coal. Sedgwick also referred to the "turf carts or coal-carts" which creaked and "jyked" in a way which must have set the teeth on edge as they were dragged "from the mountainside" to "the houses of the dalesmen in the hamlets below."

The former home of the Stationmaster sticks up from the hillside with all the emphasis of an exclamation mark. Under the eaves of the building are the mud-nests of house-martins, surely among the highest nests of this breed in the land. The Holmes family when referring to the Coal Road used to talk about going to the Klondyke. Rest your elbows on a parapet of the bridge and look at the Victorian gothic station buildings (now privatised) and, across the track, a platform with a waiting room of a simple type. Dent signal box has gone, being ripped apart, the wooden parts being put to the torch. The stone cabin remains. In clear weather, it is possible to trace the line southwards to the viaducts of Arten Gill and Dent Head.

Dodderham Moss has now been swaddled by conifers, which impart a gloomy Backwoods appearance to the environs of Rise Hill Tunnel. The rest is a desolate area, though in spring the soulful whistle of the golden plover is heard from peaty land where the bird runs with mincing steps between tussocks of ling or *Nardus stricta*. A meadow pipit, in its song flight, descends like a shuttlecock, with wings and tail feathers held out rigidly. Under its name of Galloway Gate, it was an important road for packhorse traffic. Droves of cattle were brought this way en route from Scotland to the North Country grazings, where they were fattened up for sale to butchers in the fast-growing industrial towns of the North. Some cattle were taken on the hoof as far as Smithfield in London.

The high, rounded fells, which are like waves in a petrified sea, must have daunted Young Sharland, the Tasmanian surveyor who was entrusted with the job of planning an acceptable route for the Settle-Carlisle. Sharland was mentioned by F S Williams, in his history of the Midland Railway, the writing of which extended into Settle-Carlisle "railway time". In Centenary year, several of us were researching the construction period and looking for confirmation that Sharland was not just a figment of a writer's imagination when, at my home, a telephone rang. An Antipodean voice said: "Say—my name's Sharland!" Here was a Tasmanian relative of the surveyor. He told us a little about the distinguished surveyor. The young man who fixed the line of the Settle-Carlisle was not in good health; he retired before the railway was built and died in Torquay.

Many of the old farmhouses have been sold to off-comers and the land amalgamated to form more viable units. The cattle, once almost entirely of the Shorthorn breed, were phased out in favour of the Friesian, and then of the beef types, which were ranched. Swaledale and Dales-bred sheep roam the fells. Dentdale was, until local government reorganisation in 1974, a half-forgotten dale, populated by a scattering of indomitable folk.

The Railway Cometh

FOR SEVEN years, the head of Dentdale was in a turmoil. The Midland route to Scotland was to be a no-nonsense route, not deviating for hill or gorge. Contractors faced what a local newspaper reporter summed up as ''a hostile countryside, a sullen or capricious workforce and climatic excesses.'' Contract No.1, awarded to W H Ashwell (and later taken over by the Midland itself) included a trio of mighty works—Ribblehead Viaduct, Blea Moor Tunnel and Dent Head viaduct. Messrs Benton and Woodiwiss secured Contract No 2 and immediately applied themselves to the heaviest work—to the construction of Arten Gill Viaduct and tunnelling through the eastern end of Rise Hill, the fell separating Dentdale from Garsdale. At this stage, no one worried about providing a station for Dent (which was, indeed, not built until after traffic was running).

In 1869, the legalities about land purchase for the Settle-Carlisle were completed. Stakes were driven into the ground to mark the area secured for railway-building. (It would be necessary slyly to move some of the fences back when the fluidity of the glacial clay was revealed!). What passed for roads in the dale country were churned up by the movement of heavy equipment. With a shortage of lodging accommodation, the Contractors provided wooden huts—the celebrated "shanty towns"—so that men could live near their work. The district became the resort of hard drinking, coarse-speaking workers drawn from every point of the compass and bearing outlandish nicknames such as Leeds Polly and Policeman Jack.

For months, there was little to see. In the gills, during the early period of viaduct-building, shafts had to be dug (to a depth of up to sixty feet in Arten Gill) to locate bedrock. For the protracted work of excavating tunnels, it was vital to get tramways to the fell-tops, to set up vertical steam engines and a few huts for the workers and begin the digging of deep shafts to the appropriate depth. Each shaft would open up two headings in which the miners might work. The shafts would also be needed for tunnel ventilation.

Quarries were opened out. It was mainly limestone. A quarry at Kell provided good stone for culverts. At Arten Gill and Dent Head, John Crossley and his engineers drew on outcrops of that hard, fine, strikingly fossilised limestone which, when neatly cut and polished, became Dent Marble. There were two types—black and grey. In the days when they were exploited and exported for the building trade, the pieces were removed from their ancient beds using crowbars. Explosives would have rendered the "marble" useless. The blocks had been sawn into appropriate sizes using a moving bar and the abrasive action of sand and water. The railway workers invaded Arten Gill when the great days of quarrying were over. They saw remains of High Mill, which had been powered by an enormous wheel. The mill was devoted to woollens for half a century and was then converted into a "marble mill".

The coming of the railway to Dent benefited the Marble trade—for a time. The chimney pieces and other products could not be despatched more cheaply than was the case when the horse and cart was being used. But—and it was a big "but'—Italian marbles were being introduced. The Arten Gill firm polished rough slabs of Italian marble when it was found these were being preferred to the local product. By 1900, however, the Marble industry was just an item for the history book. One of the reminders was the marble fireplace surround at Dent station.

It is worth noting that in 1835, William George Armstrong, a solicitor from Newcastle who had just become associated with an armaments firm, arrived in the upper dale with his new bride for their honeymoon. He had intended to spend any spare time angling but he became fascinated by the marble-works in Arten Gill. Taking a close look at the water-wheel, he jotted down measurements and calculations and reckoned that it was operating at only about five per cent of its optimum power. Back in Newcastle, he conducted research into the more efficient use of hydraulic power. It was the take-off point for an industry which became renowned as Armstrongs of Tyneside.

Welsh masons were at a premium in the task of building viaducts. The piers of those which would transform the deep gills of upper Dentdale emerged from behind light timber staging, with a jenny or crane placed on a movable platform extending from one stage to the other. The details were given to F S Williams, the Midland historian, by John Crossley, who said that materials were wound up either by hand or steam power and were moved along until they could be lowered on to the exact position they were to occupy. ''As soon as the masonry is built up to the height of the gantry, a fresh lift of timber is put on, the crane is raised to a new height, and so the work is continued.''

The pieces of dressed marble which were so moved to form the piers and arches of Arten Gill viaduct totalled an

DENT STATION, SITUATED
AT MONKEY BECK

estimated 50,000 tons. Williams heard that one stone in the viaduct measured fourteen feet by six feet and was a foot thick. Its weight was more than eight tons. The masons were chilled and buffeted by the weather. When the arches of a viaduct were turned, local people would stare with drooping jaws at what had been accomplished.

It must have been fascinating to see the activity on Rise Hill. Coal for the steam engines was brought up on the tramway. Material dislodged in the headings was drawn up the shafts in huge iron buckets, to be dumped as large spoil heaps. Down below, the crump of explosions in the confined space must have been a torment to the miners. They were using dynamite, then a novelty. Sometimes a charge did not go off, and the miner could not be bothered to remove the dynamite. Later, another miner would begin drilling in the same spot and, in the delayed explosion, lose limbs or his life.

The rainfall was impressive, even by Pennine standards. The teeming, tippling precipitation affected work on the cuttings by "rendering the otherwise hard material so soft that it was totally unfit to be tipped into the bank...On this account, several cuttings had to be stopped until liberated by the fine weather." This was an allusion to boulder-clay, a sort of geological mush, which on a wet day had the consistency of Yorkshire pudding mixture and on a fine day might be rock-hard.

Dr Page, the Medical Officer of the Sedbergh and Rural Sanitary Authority, distinguished in his report between the deaths of the dalesfolk and those "among the migratory occupants of the huts at Reygill, in Garsdale, and at Black Moss and Dale Head in Dent." During the quarter ended March 31, 1874, nine deaths were recorded "at those temporary places of abode". Of two recorded deaths from typhoid fever, one had occurred at the navvy huts at Dalehead. The workers frequently stared death in the face.

One hot July day in 1870, blue-black clouds gathered over the upper dale and the Grandfather of All Thunderstorms put on an audio-visual display. For two hours, water descended as though from a celestial hosepipe, though neighbouring Deepdale and the Sedbergh area were unaffected. Five miners working about forty yards inside the north portal of Blea Moor tunnel found themselves standing in swirling water which deepened by the second. The partly-excavated tunnel was almost filled to the roof. One of the rescuers, a young man, swam up the tunnel to where the water was about two feet from the roof and found a miner standing on a mound with only his nose and the top of his head out of the water. The young man returned for a piece of wood to form a raft. The miner was more dead than alive when rescued.

The storm damaged the railway works. On Contract No.1, Mr Ashwell was left lamenting the loss of timber and railway plant. At Cowgill, Messrs Benton & Woodiwiss discovered that their stored baulks of timber—the type used as scaffolding for viaduct and bridgework—had been swept away. Water which coursed through the hut occupied by Mr Metcalfe, the horseman, bore away his cash-box, furniture and some of his clothes. If rain was not falling, then there might be an unexpected slip of earth. In October, 1870, one such fall took the life of William Howe. At his funeral, the coffin was carried into Cowgill Church by eight of his fellow workmen, all dressed in white slops and black trousers and caps.

The "big works" at the head of Dentdale needed a small army of workers. Almost in the shadow of the emergent viaduct, a shanty town grew from a nucleus of typical contractors' huts, which were long and of simple structure. Another building became a shop, one of a string of stores owned by Messrs Burgoyne and Cocks, who were making a fortune as provision dealers. At Batty Green (Ribblehead) they had a brick oven in which 2,000 loaves a day were produced, to be distributed to their local shops by horse and cart. The firm also maintained a large "butching shop" at Ribblehead.

The navvies were rough but, generally, law-abiding. The root of their trouble was off-duty boredom and the harsh conditions in which they lived, which caused some of them to drink excessively. Drink supplied without the knowledge of the Revenue was freely available in some of the huts. Revenue officers and the police snooped at night, peering through windows, waiting for a navvy to pay for his ale. Cases of theft or assault were dealt with harshly, with banishment to the House of Correction at Wakefield. One way of meeting the illicit drink problem was to increase the number of official outlets. In 1870, the Sedbergh Bench approved applications to sell drink by Mr R Bragg, of Bridge-end, Dent; Mr T Squires of Dent; W Boaden, of the Stone House, Dent; and Mr C Harris of Dent Head.

However, in that same year, James Oxendale, of "the Railway Huts, at Dent Head", was charged with having sold a quantity of beer to a man named Curley, without having a licence so to do. The sale was proved by a navvy named Pugh, "who appeared in the box with a recently inflicted black eye". He had seen the defendant's wife, in the presence of the defendant, supply Curley with a pint of ale and receive payment for a quart with which he had been previously supplied. The defendant's legal representative claimed that the story was trumped up in revenge for the defendant's wife having turned him away from his lodgings. Oxendale was fined 20s, and costs.

The Christian influence was brought to bear on the wilder elements in the shanty towns. In addition to the ministrations of Anglican clergymen at Chapel-le-Dale, Cowgill and Dent, the Midland Company approached the Bradford City Mission and missionaries were appointed to serve at Ribblehead and Kirkby Stephen. Quaker ladies instructed shanty-town families in the skills of hand-knitting. Methodist lay preachers "took the Gospel" to the peripheral areas. One Methodist preacher, provided with a horse and cart by Mr Ashwell, chose to venture into the wilderness on an August Sunday, 1872, when (as the visitor recorded) "hill and dale, heath and meadow, all looked as charming as in a morning in May".

On the Settle-Carlisle, no one worked on the Sabbath. At Dent Head, "the workmen who gathered round were in their shirt sleeves, some smoking, one holding a cat and another a dog. Many of these men are very fond of animals and consequently set their affections on either birds, fowls, dogs, cats, &c...Though Saturday night was pay night, it was pleasant to see that none of them was under the influence of drink." They provided the visitors with refreshments. At Dent Head, Christian witness resulted in a hut being made available as a church, which was furnished with wooden forms. A Reading Room was provided. Mr Duffy, manager of the works, gave support to communal activities such as Penny Readings and concerts. Thomas Burgoyne, provision merchant, usually recited a "poetic effusion of his own composing".

The Methodist witness was least effective at Tunnel Huts, on the draughty hilltop. Not surprisingly, some of the men, relaxing after their mole-like existence in the bowels of Blea Moor, turned to the bottle. On their first visit, the Methodists sang a portion of a hymn and the preacher said a few words. Religious tracts were distributed. And then they were off, on the road to Jericho (another shanty), stopping briefly to chat to a trader who was "plying his trade on the Sabbath Day" He charged the Methodists with profiting from their own Sunday activities, but "fortunately he was under a mistake."

Messrs Benton and Woodiwiss, having the daunting task of bridging the "deep and rugged" Arten Gill, with its sixty feet waterfall, were soon being retarded by constant breakages of the machinery used for lifting the blocks into position. There was an urgency in doing the work where ten lofty piers were needed. The highest pier would be 103 ft at the springing and twenty-six feet from there to rail level, the base of a pier being 38 feet by 15 feet and that of one of the two "block" piers measuring forty-two feet by twenty-eight feet. In 1872, when no sand could be found in the district, John Crossley (the Midland's resident engineer) suggested that burnt clay should be ground up with lime—a compound which proved to be a good substitute. The lime and clay were burnt on the spot. A steam engine was used to grind and mix the mortar.

Between Artengill and Rise Hill, the terrain was steep and peaty. Everywhere was the sound of running water in runnels and becks. As related, a good source of stone was found to the east of Kell Beck. The foundations of an occupation bridge, one leading to the moorland grazings above, were sunk thirty feet but, the engineers being unhappy, a further

KELL BECK CULVERT

twenty-five feet was excavated and piles installed. For just one of several large cuttings, 95,000 cubic yards of material were removed. Kell Beck culvert was built as a succession of steps—"from twenty to thirty breaks in the descending underground watercourse. . . The repeating falls of the mountain stream have a pleasant effect on both the eye and the ear."

Between the Coal Road and Rise Hill were "many very deep cuttings of black shale, bog earth and rock." Material drawn from the cutting near Monkey Beck amounted to 150,000 cubic yards, all of which (and more) was swallowed up by an embankment of awesome height between here and Rise Hill Tunnel. Constant dumping of material taken from the tunnel and from cuttings led to the formation of an embankment with a maxium depth of a hundred feet. A culvert to cater for the Cow Gill Beck had a length of 540 feet and became the largest on the Contract, the beck emerging from a Gothic-style arch sixteen feet high and ten feet wide. The retaining wall was built to a height of fifty feet.

Rise Hill (or Black Moss) Tunnel, stretching 1,213 yards from Rise Hill to Mossdale Moor, was worked from the two headings and two shafts, each 170 feet deep. About 120 miners blasted their way through "solid and hard rock, some of which weighed more like iron than stone." Eventually, the tunnel was arched with masonry throughout. A visitor who was lowered in a skip entered a man-made cavern where "there is something unearthly in the sounds and appearances of mining operations." Here were dimly-burning candles, "like twinkling stars on a hazy night". Drills were being twirled beneath the terrible force of big hammers wielded by stalwart men. At each stroke, there was a "hac-hac or half sepulchral groan".

Rise Hill had its own shanty, formed as usual of wooden huts, set on the moor at an elevation of about 1,130 ft. The huts, and another cluster down by the Garsdale road, were the temporary home or workplace of about 350 workers. The two places were connected by a 600 yard long tramway, operated by a steam winding engine and endless rope. Around the head of Shaft No.1, in the summer of 1872, a visitor saw a blacksmith's shop, eight huts, miners' cabin, store-room and engine-house. The engine, a double cylinder type of twenty horse power, blew air into the tunnel and lifted the excavated material. At No. 2 shaft were a blacksmith's shop, a general storehouse, a mortar mill and five huts. A steam engine of twenty-five horse power provided power for trucks on the tramway, being used for drawing up from Garsdale the coal, provisions and railway material required for the tunnelling.

At the bottom of the hill stood numerous huts, a weighing machine, stabling for ten horses and a blacksmith's shop. One of the more unusual items carried on the tramway was a barrel of beer, belonging to Charles Jones, a miner. Though he had been told by a railway engineer that no beer should be sold in the huts without a licence, Jones insisted on moving the ale. When he threated to murder the engineer who cautioned him, Jones was whisked before the magistrates who ordered him to keep the peace for six months.

David Page, Medical Officer of Health, explained a larger-than-normal death rate in the quarter ending September, 1874, as being three fatilities "from the accidental overturning of trucks" on the tramway. Carelessness was the main reason for such accidents. Dr Page added: "As similar accidents, although unattended by fatal results, have since occurred at this very place, I would recommend steps to be taken with a view to preventing the habitual use of these dangerous truckways for the purposes of ascent and descent of the steep hill by dozens of the wives and children of the navvies employed there."

The Medical Officer then got on to the topic of the poor standards of sanitation at the Dent Head hutment. Wooden structures which were occupied by navvies, miners, their families and lodgers were "clustered upon a patch of bogland made almost untraversable by reason of the state of puddle it is in from surface water and refuse matters thrown out immediately from the doorways. Planks laid over this quagmire and stepping-stones afford access to some of the huts. There is no vestage of drainage save the open trenches cut around the walls of the huts to protect them from inundation. Overcrowding is the rule, and the cubic space to each occupant in the sleeping apartments is very much below 300 ft, the minimum required for the maintenance of health. In one hut I noticed five bedsteads jammed so tightly together that the sleepers in reaching the furthest beds must necessarily clamber over the others."

Amazingly, "this eminently vagrant population" was quite healthy, "a circumstance less due to the conditions in which they live than to the abundance of substantial food and the fresh air of the daytime, which enable them to escape the bad effects of an atmosphere vitiated by the exhalations from their persons at night." If infectious disease did break out, the whole district would be threatened and as the railway work was likely to continue for two or three years yet, Dr Page insisted that the interior of each hut should be periodically lime-washed and the soil drained, even by open trenches or tiles. There should also be a restriction on the number of lodgers. Finally, a hut, complete with a store of disinfectants such as carbolic acid powder, might be made available for any infectious cases. (Smallpox was a major medical concern in 1871).

The shanties were awash with drink being supped without the knowledge of the Revenue. Any confiscated barrels of beer were breached. Some workers who intercepted a supply of whisky being collected from an inn for Mr Ashwell, the contractor, remarked that if whisky was not to be kept in the huts, then they did not see any objection in transferring it to their stomachs! Police and the Revenue men snooped round the huts at night.

Bare-fisted fighting was a Sunday attraction in quiet places. William Williams, a 23-year-old miner, and John Atkins, better known as Policeman Jack, who quarrelled while working at Rise Hill, found the old grudge rankled after they had moved to Blea Moor. Atkins challenged Williams to a fight he did not seem to want. A flurry of bare fists ended in the death of Williams. The fight took place near Newby Head on a Sunday morning in August, 1874. A silent crowd of spectators occupied the periphery and testified that the two men were sober and during the fight they used only their fists, not their feet. After four rounds of fighting, during which they proved to be well matched, both men collapsed.

Williams died from his injuries and Atkins fled in the direction of Ingleton. The Dent Head policeman followed his trail as far as Thornton-in-Lonsdale. At the inquest, held in the School at Dent Head, witnesses testified to the fairness of the fight and Dr Griffiths affirmed that death had been caused by blood infused on the brain from a bruise on the scalp. The jury returned a verdict of manslaughter. The absent Atkins was committed to take his trial at the next Assizes.

In May, 1874, "on one of the desolate and heath-clad moors, called Rise Hill, above Dent and Garsdale", Robert Nicholson, whose job was helping to fill trucks in the tunnel with displaced rock, took his own life. Illness had lowered his will to live. When he was heard threatening to cut his throat with his knife, a man was appointed to look after him. One evening, Robert went to the water closet which stood a short distance from the huts. When he did not re-appear in a reasonable time, the door was forced and he was found to have carried out his threat. His throat was cut. He was "gasping in the agony of death".

A man who rode in a contractor's locomotive from Kirkby Stephen to Settle in October, 1875, had the company of Mr Hay, manager for Messrs Benton and Woodiwiss. The engine gave a cheerful toot as it entered Rise Hill Tunnel, now almost finished. About two-thirds of the arching was of brick and stone and the rest solid rock. "At intervals, the arching is strengthened by steel ribs. In different parts of the tunnel, one passed under stages where the bricklayers were quietly performing their daily task." The Cowgill embankment at the south end of the tunnel impressed the visitor by its immensity and the way it spanned one of the deepest and roughest gills on the line. At Cowgill, where there is slight curve to the south-east, the engine emerged from the deep cuttings to give its passengers a view of "the beautiful dale of Dent", the summits of the hills being crested with mist. There was an agreeable change between the "darkness and rumbling noise of the tunnel" and "the winding of the valley, the course of the river Dee, the green slopes from the hills and the snug homesteads of the people encircled with trees."

The engine continued to Dent Head viaduct, which had been completed for some time. They saw men dismantling empty huts. A fog detonator sounded a caution in Blea Moor Tunnel. The driver reduced the speed of the engine. ''Shortly we came to a number of workmen whose dimly burning candles made the deep excavation look more gloomy...On the south side of the tunnel a few cottages were being built for signalmen and other employees.''

THE LAND PLAN RELATING
TO DENT HEAD VIADUCT

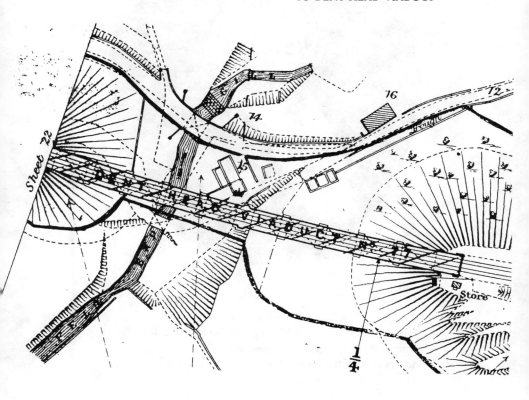

James Allport, General Manager of the Midland Railway from 1860 until 1880. He presided over the company's affairs during the protracted and expensive construction of the Settle-Carlisle railway.

Steam on the Drag

The prolonged 15-mile struggles that trains had to make to climb into the fells from either direction made it a gruelling test. An engine with a boiler that was reluctant to boil was soon in trouble.

Colin Walker, 1972.

GOODS traffic was operating in 1875 and in the following Spring a Kirtley locomotive (painted dark green) inaugurated the passenger service. This type of locomotive had a 2-4-0 wheel arrangement. One driver was heard to remark that the harder it was thumped, and the better it liked it! A Kirtley could do anything but talk. One short-coming was the spartan cab. The footplate men had scarcely any protection from Pennine wind and rain. I can imagine the crew, having checked that all was well, crouching in a corner of the cab at the train crossed one of the big viaducts in the teeth of a westerly gate. A second disadvantage on a gruelling route like the Settle-Carlisle was the smallness of this type, which meant that trains were invariably double-headed.

Kirtleys served the Settle-Carlisle well in its early years. They were named after Matthew Kirtley, who had become locomotive superintendent of the Midland in 1841, at the tender age of 28. He was in office for 32 years and, dying in 1873, he knew the excitement of the construction period without living long enough to see Steam on the Drag. In 1877, the livery was changed to blue-green, with a black edge and white lining. Not until 1883 was the celebrated Midland or Derby red adopted, the pick-out lines being black edged with yellow. It was said that the Midland used the colour because it was hard-wearing and thus economical! In the 1880s, R F Dilley recalled Kirtley's engine No. 809 running into the dead end at the south side of the Moorcock viaduct. "It lay there for two weeks and it needed the steam crane and three engines to pull it back up the sleepers one Sunday. This was great fun for us young lads."

The Midland was good at image-making. Announcing in 1876 that when the Settle-Carlisle was opened for passenger traffic, and that Pullman Cars would be run between London and Scotland, and vice versa, some bright member of the staff added "so that at night passengers will be able to retire to rest at one terminus and alight refreshed at the other in the morning." With its American stock, the Midland gave the rail traveller unexpected luxury. Then the drawbacks became obvious. The Pullmans, despite their novel heating system and stylish decor, were draughty and it was revealed that the Victorian passenger preferred compartments to one big open space. The Pullmans were withdrawn. The Midland, none the less, revolutionised rail travel. Wooden seats were replaced by upholstered seats. Allport, the general manager, abolished the category of second class travel.

Samuel Johnson, who was Kirtley's successor, presided over a period when Compounds were introduced to the Settle-Carlisle, meeting a need for increased power at no appreciable increase in the cost of operation. Johnson's 4-4-0s were the workhorses of the Settle-Carlisle for many years. A man whose boyhood of the 1880s was at Garsdale station loved to recall the Scots expresses and their Pullman cars, which had polished brass handles. "The Kirtley and Johnson engines in their Midland red paint looked as clean as new half-crowns." Johnson's locomotives were still working in the 1930s, by which time the increased weight of trains demanded more powerful locomotives.

The powers-that-be relegated the Compounds to lighter duties and brought in the Claughtons, which were associated with the old London and North-Western Railway. The

Claughtons, in turn, were overwhelmed by motive power devised when the locomotive superintendent of the LMS was Sir William Stanier. This was the period of the Patriots, the Jubilees and the Class 5s, all of the 4-6-0 wheel arrangement.

With regard to freight working, a single type of locomotive, the 0-6-0, sufficed for fifty years. In the right hands, it could be a nippy locomotive. Ahrons commented: "The Carlisle goods drivers were noted for the high speed at which they worked their trains. The signalmen between Carlisle and Leeds would always give the Carlisle goods drivers 'the road' even when they were within measurable distance of the following express passenger train, because the signalman knew that the goods train would keep clear, but when the Leeds goods drivers came along they were promptly shunted into the nearest siding until the passenger train had passed."

My favourite locomotive was one of the least glamorous. I refer to Bonnyface, which in my day operated on week-days from Bradford to Hawes. Why did this 4.25 p.m. passenger train from Hawes acquire the name Bonnyface? R F Dilley, son of a signalman at Hawes Junction (now Garsdale), was fond of recalling when, between the years 1886 and 1890, he attended Hawes school:

"About twelve of us had to travel from Hawes Junction in a brake van with engineers and signal and telegraph men from Settle and Horton. At that time, Mr Silcock, permanent way inspector, and Mr Slater, signal and telegraph superintendent of Settle, had a third brake carriage run from Hellifield to Hawes Junction to carry their men, who were invariably exposed to bad weather during their working day. The service proving to be a boon, it was extended to Hawes. When the service began in 1899, one of the men—delighted to see the train approaching—would say: 'Here's Bonnyface'. The name stuck and was passed down the generations."

Some Other Points of View

TURNING UP by Lea Gate, a road—or rather an apology for a road—winds up the breast of the mountain to Dent Station. The traveller who here sets "a stout heart to a stee brae" and hastens...to catch his train, had needs be encumbered with but small appurtenances of personal luggage. Once arrived on the breezy platform, he may have time to observe the provision of gigantic palisades of uplifted sleepers, intended to check the snowdrifts which at times accumulate alarmingly in this region and have been known to delay imprisoned passengers for hours. But we do not want to take the train, so, if you please, we will descend to the neighbourhood of the Dee once more.

Rev W Thompson (1910).

THE PICTURE of this proposed Alpine railway was a gloomy one, yet the whole of the obstacles have been overcome, and the line is now rendered one of the best, safest and quickest railway routes in the kingdom. In fact, a stranger to the district may apprehend nothing remarkable during his flight between Settle and Carlisle, and would hardly realise where the difficulties have been.

Harry Speight (1892).

FEW SAVE railwaymen have enjoyed the privilege of, say, standing on Dent Head viaduct to gaze down the long green miles of verdant Dent Dale...Railwaymen can tell fishermen's stories: of how once on a time the Stationmaster at Dent "tickled" his breakfast trout out of the beck that leaps down the steep hillside from Dent station to Cowgill...

Frederick W Houghton (1948).

DENT DALE is about ten miles in length. "It is," said a writer fifty years ago, "entirely surrounded with high mountains, and so difficult of access to carriages, having few openings where they can enter with safety. In this secluded spot landed property is greatly divided"...Yet in this "secluded spot", the engineer has come, and where "carriages could scarcely find a safe entry", he has laid down his paths of iron and run his mighty trains.

Frederick S Williams (1877).

Where Shall We Put The Station?

It is supposed that a station will be made near the Cowgill Coal Road. At one time it was in contemplation to make it at Dent Head. Whichever site may be fixed upon, the ascent to it will be steep and difficult.
Rambler (1875).

It is a mistake to rush up that steep road to Dent Station hard on the heels of breakfast. The road rears up like a wild thing on its hind legs, and plays havoc with one's lungs and digestion; yet in spite of the wheezing and groaning, how rich is the reward as one tops the rise!
Alfred J Brown.

WHICHEVER site was chosen, Dent station was bound to be unhandy. The first proposal, put forward in 1872, was to site the station at Dent Head. Though handy for the road, this was seven miles from Dent Town. The next proposal, for Arten Gill, was not taken seriously and in 1875 the Dent Head site was again under consideration. Mr Crossley and Mr Allport, resident engineer and general manager respectively, were asked by the construction committee to report on the site "as regards Lord Bective's offer to sell some land to the company". (This site had been chosen by Mr Punchard, agent to Lord Bective). The final choice, as noted in the construction committee minutes for November 30, 1875, was the present position by Monkey Beck, alongside the Coal Road, which twists uphill—seventeen per cent graded—and in winter frequently has drifts of snow across it.

The type of station—large, medium or small—was chosen, sensibly, according to traffic potential. There were no high

41

hopes for Dent, which was awarded small-station status, being open for public use in 1877. The Midland did give the station a spacious setting, using ground levelled on a 1 in 4 hillside. The waiting shelter on the "up" line was recessed into the hillside and a retaining wall was needed at the back of the platform.

The main group of buildings, one of the few to be set by the "down" platform, had the customary Settle-Carlisle steep-pitched roofs and decorated barge boarding. In the waiting room was a mantle to the fireplace composed of Dent Marble. Another special feature was the hood placed over each of the front windows. It was a way of cheating the weather. Around the station were good examples of Midland furniture, such as V-trap gates and fencing with the pieces of wood set diagonally to each other.

A massive four-arch overbridge (No.96) was needed to take the Coal Road over the tracks. The bridge was built entirely of brick. From it could be see the wooden signal box, a structure with a twenty-lever tumbler frame. It was brought into use on August 9, 1891. (The Box was closed on January 28, 1981). A cattle dock, with adjacent standing for two wagons, and The Dent Hotel (as a low, rugged stone-built cabin was known) were the only other structures. It had been proposed to build two houses for railway servants but this was not done. A five-ton crane was strategically sited beside the siding leading to the cattle dock.

Goods facilities were slight, based on this one siding, a reception area for the vast quantities of South Yorkshire coal which replaced, on local hearths, the thin brittle stuff mined in the Yoredale Series of Rocks, at the modest pits beside the Coal Road.

Dent conformed to the overall Midland style. The architect ignored local traditions and settled for what became known as Midland Gothic. Being used throughout, it gave the Settle-Carlisle a sense of unity. There was just the variation of materials used—basically limestone in North Ribblesdale and

New Red Sandstone in the Eden Valley. The main building was composed of a double gable, separated by a central porch through which access was available through doors in a screen of wood and glass. On the side away from the platform was a projecting central gable. From the main structure was an extension with a lower roofline. Among the non-standard buildings at Dent was a hut used as a weigh-office.

When a Lancashire school had a lease of the buildings as a field centre, someone explored the loft and discovered it had been used for many years for the storage of files. They had been forgotten. As Cecil Sanderson remarks, most of the Stationmasters at Dent were not there for long. They were promoted—and went joyfully away to lower and warmer climes.

A BLACK 5 RUSHES THROUGH DENT

The men from Holbeck at Leeds, being concerned with passenger trains, got the best of the locomotives and the best of the coal. A driver from another depot remarked: "We used to call coaches 'mahoganies', though they were painted. 'He's on mahoganies', we'd say as a Holbeck train went by..."

Thirsty Expresses

PASSENGER traffic reached its peak of frequency in the Edwardian twilight. Three daytime expresses from St Pancras carried through coaches for both Glasgow and Edinburgh. Complex arrangements, and an agreement between the Midland and the Lancashire and Yorkshire Railway, used the Settle-Carlisle for trains emanating from Liverpool Exchange and Manchester Victoria to Glasgow and Edinburgh. There were night trains, too. At his home overlooking the line at Settle, the tycoon John Delaney, who made his brass through importing coal and exporting lime from his several Dales quarries, became agitated if the Scots Express was late on its nocturnal run. He would rouse the household and was only placated when the train, with a shriek of escaping steam, went by, storming the Drag.

Dent was on a relatively level stretch of track. The main haul from Settle reached a peak in Blea Moor tunnel. North of Rise Hill, where the line was level for a spell, the engineers fitted water-troughs between the lines so that trains might refill their tenders without stopping. Water for the troughs came from a dam made on the fellside. It is said that when the dam was constructed, the man in charge—anxious to save the Midland some money—made an inadequate mix for the cement, with the result that when the stream which had been diverted was put back into its original course, the dam leaked like a colander.

Two serious pre-1914 accidents on the Settle-Carlisle occurred between Garsdale (then known as Hawes Junction) and Aisgill, a few miles north of Dent. The first accident occurred on Christmas Eve, 1910, when two light engines which had piloted two up-trains early that day awaited a signal to return

45

to Carlisle. The signals were pulled off at 5-44 a.m., and the light trains began their fateful journey. The overworked signalman had forgotten about them and the signals were for the St Pancras-Glasgow express, which was double-headed. The express soon overhauled the two engines as they came off Lunds viaduct. The collision occurred with the express travelling at 65 miles an hour. The wooden, gas-lit coaches were consumed by fire.

Then, on the night of September 2, 1913, a southbound express, a sleeper, ran short of steam because of the poor quality of the coal and because there had been no available pilot. Needless to say, the weather was at its Pennine worst, with wind and rain. The train came to a halt just north of Aisgill summit. The crew of a following express from Scotland, also labouring through the poor quality of the coal in its tender, over-ran the signals at Mallerstang and collided with the back of the standing express. Again, there was fire and fourteen lives were lost.

After the 1914-18 war, the Settle-Carlisle handled comparatively little passenger traffic. In the early years of the 1939-45 war, bridges were strengthened to permit the use of greater power, as represented by the Royal Scot 4-6-0's. In the 1950s, there were five trains—three by day, two by night—each way. Most of them were "through" trains. It was a time when Bishop Treacy was active with his camera. He secured a stunning picture of a Rebuilt Scot (Royal Engineer) against the classic view from Dent, with the fell and snow fencing on the left and, far away to the right, the silver-grey form of Arten Gill viaduct.

Coal, Cattle and Coffins

IN 1873, before the entire rail link from Settle to Carlisle was complete, coal was being transported from the south to Dent Head for farmers who had previously had to move it by horse and cart from Sedbergh. Coal merchants did make their rounds, but business was never brisk among those who lived near the railway. There was coal, coal, coal—as much as anyone wanted! It used to roll off the engines. Every platelayer's cabin had a big heap of coal composed of cobs picked up on the track. Further up the line, an old platelayer stood up a dead pheasant in his garden and the footplate men could not resist throwing coal in the hope of hitting it. Dent dealt with a vast range of goods and—in November, 1887—a corpse was consigned by rail the fifty-six miles from Leeds to Dent, at a charge of a shilling a mile; it cost the bereaved family £2.16.

The aforementioned files of old documents in the loft at Dent station included counterfoils for this item and also for first-class rail tickets, indicating that in 1883 you might travel from Dent to Hawes for 1s.11d; to Blackburn for 7s.2d; to Northallerton for 5s.11d and to Liverpool for 12s.1d. In 1896, the Dent station staff handled a mowing machine, twenty loads of corn, six bags of sugar, four buckets of lard and innumerable loads of basic slag, in 2 cwt bags.

Fine details are available for goods received in the old Midland days, between 1896 and 1902. A major importer, J Brunskill of Dent, received from Butterworths of Kendal bags of sugar and maize, buckets of lard, many loads of corn and boxes of candles. Leeds Phosphate Works despatched to Brunskills bags of slag (75 bags at a time). Other items noted are "1 cwt xx Pale Soap" a butter-worker and a touchstone.

The Kendal firm of Butterworths also dealt with J Greenbank and Batty & Son. W & J Bairstow, of Skipton, supplied maize and flat corn to R Raw, a more distant supplier U Woodhead of Bradford, directed 10 bags of cement to Dent for delivery to J Bayne and G Hadfield & Co of Liverpool sent 60 bags of slag which were distributed among local farmers—T Dixon, J Parrington, E Baines, W Lambert, J Allen, T Sedgwick, R Burton, T Oversby and J Parkinson.

Towards the end of the nineteeth century, large quantities of basic slag arrived at Dent station. The Union Feeding Company of Liverpool, supplied a bag of meal, casks of meal and bags of cattle cake to a quartet of Dent farmers—R Burton, R Goth, J Mason and J D Conder. In 1899, A Bell & Son of Lancaster sent a crate of glass, via the Midland, to M Greenwood and another crate to J Middleton, both of Dent. From H Brown & Son of Luton came 4 tons 8 cwt of cut slates, which had been bought by J Baynes and the firm of Harrison and Co., of Chesterfield, consigned a truck of coal to W Mason.

By 1899, it was possible to judge some rapid changes in local farming by the imported items. Basic slag was being spread widely, with some farmers ordering two tons, the majority requiring a ton, and Mr Mason of Southwaite, being content with half a ton. Butterworths were still supplying Brunskills of Dent with boxes of soap and buckets of lard. In 1900, Farrers of Kendal had become prime suppliers of slag, in quantities ranging from half a ton to three tons. It was delivered to T Sedgwick of Spicegill, T Dixon of Belge End, T Capstick of Broad Field, R Tatham of Dent, H Staveley of High Hall, G Oversby of Hall Bank, R Dixon and T Pinch of Deep Dale, Staveley of Hawcross and R Oversby of Bank Land. Slag was also being received in bags from Langdale Brothers of Newcastle, consignments of 16 bags each being delivered to Dawson of Mill Beck, Booth of Bigside, Fawcett of Throstle Hall and Mason of Hole House.

In December, 1900, Manby of Skipton transported a kitchen range by rail to Dent for Mr Hodgson of Dent and in the following Spring another old-established Dales firm, Dawson of Settle, forwarded to Dent Station a stove and pipe, which were eventually fitted at the Dent home of J Mattinson. Also sent were five grates for Mrs Chapman of Coventree, some spouting and two bedsteads required by W Oversby, of Cage Farm, and a mowing machine for Mr Hodgson, of Dent. He dealt in agricultural machinery, for that summer four other mowing machines were delivered to him. In January, 1901, a mangle was off-loaded at Dent station for Mrs Bentham of Mill Beck. Tons of slag were being consigned to Dent farmers by 1902. Butterworths of Kendal continued to send bulk supplies of groceries to Brunskills and Batty & Son.

John Earl and Jim Greenbank, two coal merchants, were "terribly at variance with one another." In those days, the horse was master of the dusty road. Using a horse and cart, a coal dealer could make up to four journeys a day, a task demanding the best from a horse, which had to struggle to keep its hooves on the road. The journey up to the station was with an empty cart. On the way back, the horse must learn how to hold back the laden cart to control its descent. The average load was eight hundredweights. With the brakes partly applied, a cart squeaked all the way down the hill.

Jack Sedgwick used to relate that most of the coal came from Haigh Pit. "Sometimes you loaded a cart out o'wagins and sometimes off t'ground. Coal cost about ls.3d a cwt. We burnt coal at home quite a lot. We got a few peats, but they wean't a big success." The last carters recalled by Jack Sedgwick were Bill Moorby and David Raw. They raced each other up the hill. He who arrived first had the lucrative job of collecting parcels which had arrived by rail and had to be delivered, for a fee, in the dale.

During the 1926 General Strike, when no coal reached Dent by rail, an Ingleton man dug coal from a seam outcropping in the bed of the Greta and carted the coal up Kingsdale and over the top to Dent, where he proposed to make a good profit. As he arrived, news came that the Strike was over. Then he could scarcely give away his coal. In the 1930s, Len Haygarth, who was the coal merchant at Dent station, drove to work on a motor-bike at a time when not many men in the dale possessed one. He used the little hut near the weighbridge. The old-time Dent carters were made redundant with the appearance of a motor wagon owned by R H Sanderson. "He carried owt." The first load he bore from Dent was baled hay. Jack recalls it was so loose he had to borrow every rope at the station to tie it down.

In the period 1938-45, when Sandy was Stationmaster, goods from the scattered farms and houses, and any deliveries, were handled mainly by Rowland Sanderson (no relation) who coped astonishingly well with the Coal Road when it was dusted with snow and plated with ice. "I've seen him struggling like mad, putting all sorts of things under the wheels, reversing a bit, then trying again. Sometimes, it's been a bit nerve-racking for him when driving down the hill."

Working on a smaller scale, and with horse and cart, was David Raw, who shifted coal in bulk. Sometimes, after David had a rough journey up the hill, he was "flaked out" on arriving at the station. He used to tell Sandy about a previous Stationmaster's off-handedness. "I'll never forget coming up that hill on a bad slippery road. My horse was struggling to get up. And I got within sight of the yard gates—it was just before five o'clock when they were supposed to be closed—when who should be standing at the side was the Stationmaster. He just slammed the gate, locked it and walked to his house."

There were three categories of parcels—Paid, Paid Home and To Pay. "It could be a complicated system when it came to clearing accounts. Old David Raw would turn up with his horse and cart and say: 'Have you got owt for t'dale then?' I'd reply: 'Yes, I've a few parcels that'll suit you.' David had a load of coal and I didn't want to give him any big parcels that would fall off. He got the smaller parcels. He would say, of any awkward parcel: 'I don't want that one'. It was left to the always-affable Rowland to attend to it. He never complained but sometimes he had a wry smile on his face when I told him what David had said about the awkward parcels.

"They were tough guys. And they were adaptable. Rowland had wagon loads—straw, potatoes and the like—for the farmers. He even took consignments of Danish butter from the station to Dinsdale's shop at Dent, where it was mixed with local butter to improve the quality, Danish butter being supposedly the best in the world. Old Mr Hodgson, the blacksmith at Dent Town, took deliveries of metal of various kinds and sizes, for besides shoeing horses he also made wrought-iron gates and the bits and pieces needed by farmers. A lot of people were frightened to death of him, but he was always a gentleman with me. We'd sit round an old stove, when I'd presented my accounts. And he'd say: 'Have a drop of whisky'." Dent station did not have major facilities for handling stock. The line as a whole was handling much of the Scottish cattle trade. As early as 1876, "a large number of cattle and sheep is being sent into this district from Scotland, and the two companies—the North British and the Glasgow and South Western—send all their trade by the Midland route, as this line affords them a through route for their traffic destined south, and they are no longer under the power of the London and North-Western Railway, who always gave preference to the Caledonian traffic..."

Much of this trade occurred at Garsdale when it was known as Hawes Junction. The sheep dealers—Willy Pratt, T T Iveson and Willy Moore (senior and junior)—went to Scotland and purchased thousands of sheep, which were transported to the Dales in a special train. The sheep were unloaded and turned out on Garsdale Common which, being strange ground, was followed by hours of anxious bleating. R F Dilley recalled that when these special trains were notified, the platelayers had to dig two or three graves as there were always some sheep to bury because they had been overcrowded in the vans. "Above the station, dozens of sheep have been interred."

Dent dealt mainly with sheep, though a dealer called W I Bentham drove a few *bee-asts* up the hill. Farmers consigning cattle to Hawes auction paid 7s.6d (37p) from Dent. Calves in sacks were sent to Leeds on passenger trains. Tups purchased by Dentdale farmers at Kirkby Stephen travelled in the guard's van. Cecil Sanderson, who came to Dent in the late 1930s, recalls that a farmer wishing to despatch cattle or sheep paid for a part load, a medium load or a full load. Different rates applied. A part-load was carried in a section of the van which was partitioned off. A cute farmer, having mentioned to the station staff he had a part load, did his best to slip in a few more animals undetected. "Hey—it's a medium load already," one of the staff would say. The farmer would simply reply: "Oh—I med a mistake," and in the end was persuaded to pay for a 'medium' load ".

The aforementioned Billy Bentham exported and also imported stock. Ever ready to make a penny or two, he also dealt in grain, hay and straw, which he consigned from Dent to Haverton Hill, in the North East, via Garsdale and the Wensleydale line. In the days before a Dales farmer might benefit from the high mobility provided by a motor vehicle, the railway was the handiest means of transport for his stock. Sandy, as Stationmaster, attended sheep sales held near the Sportsman's Arms, in the confident hope of being able to arrange for stock to be moved by rail. He joined the agents in the pub. When a batch of sheep was to be driven up the hill to the station, Sandy would signal from near the pub to the station, indicating how many animals were on their way and in which direction—north or south—they were to go. If the signalman was busy, and unable to keep an eye on Sandy's arm-waving form far below, the message did not get through.

Trespassing sheep were not uncommon. The horned sheep of the Pennines were like kangeroos, being able to jump virtually any wall if they set their minds to it. Lineside grass was sweeter than the benty stuff on the fellside. The business of removing the sheep was normally left to the ganger and lengthmen. If a trespassing sheep was killed, the farmers of the Dent area just accepted it. They did not scream for compensation. "Very often, we'd find the wall was down anyway; the sheep had wandered through the gap."

There was compensation for a farmer in winter, when a fierce wind stripped a goods train of its wagon sheets and sent them far and wide, a windfall in a literal sense for a farmer in need of something to cover a stack. Sandy observes: "A train would emerge from a tunnel to be met by a howling gale. It would break the cords, whip off the sheets and they would fly in the air like parachutes. They seemed to go for miles. At Dent station, a goods train which was at a bad angle to the wind would lose a number of sheets. Sandy has known when the roof of a box-van was torn off outside Blea Moor Tunnel. "A van must have had a weak roof because the wind seemed to have no difficulty in ripping it away. Unfortunately, when the roof came back to earth, it hit one of the platelayers and killed him. It was as easy as that."

DENT STATION IN SNOWTIME, 1983

Jenny Holme
1987

The Stationmasters

WHEN Bill Nicholson was the Stationmaster at Dent, and some ninety trains a day—"thirty a shift"—used the line, he was fond of relating that one of his porters did not have a uniform for a protracted period. "I git yan after," he said. The Stationmaster was provided with a house. This porter was living at home, or—as he said—he would not have been able to afford to work for the railway. He worked forty-eight hours spread over six days and was paid the far from princely sum of "thirty-eight bob a week".

Cecil Sanderson, Stationmaster from 1938 until 1945, had begun his railway career in 1929, aged sixteen, when he was appointed porter-signalman on the Furness line. In the following year, he went to Apperley Bridge, stayed there one night—that was all—and three days later was at Leeds Wellington, as a summer station lampman in charge of the Lamp Office. "Two of us had to do all the lamps—headlamps, tail lamps—of the trains through the twenty-four hours." At his next posting, Oakworth, Sandy met Margaret (who would become his wife). Thence to Selside as a Class 6 signalman, from October, 1934, to June, 1935. It was his first encounter with the Settle-Carlisle line.

Selside came under Horton. Sandy worked a shift at the Dent Head box on a temporary basis. It was December, 1934, and a landslide had occurred in the cutting near Arten Gill viaduct. Half the eastern fell seemed to come down, blocking both lines and demolishing an aqueduct across the cutting. Sandy, while cycling to Dent Head from Selside, to help out at the signal box, recalls a change of weather at Ribblehead, where he was brought to a halt by wind-driven snow and thereupon had to carry his bike. He abandoned the machine near Dent Head, simply lowering it over a wall, where—such was the snowfall—it would be covered over in five minutes. Dent Head, on the south side of Arten Gill, was an intermediate box kept busy by quite heavy traffic.

For the Arten Gill blockage of 1934-5, hundreds of plate-layers worked in shifts, night and day, on both sides of the obstruction. On the south side, ballast wagons were filled, then taken to Ribblehead viaduct and the contents dumped over the parapets. At night time, the only illumination consisted of paraffin hand lamps. "Work went on for over a fort-night and the men worked in atrocious conditions. One day, I opened the door of the Dent Head box and it was caught by an easterly gale, swinging me against the protecting bars on the landing at the top of the steps. I managed to hang on but could not breathe very well. They dragged me back inside the box and used the old Dent revival technique, beginning with a cup of OXO. Mr Hibbert, the Operating Superintendent from Derby, who supervised the work came back into Sandy's life in 1935 when, as he worked at Heysham Harbour station as Signalman Class 5, he suggested Sandy should apply for training as a Stationmaster. In due course, two vacancies came up at the same time—Grange-over-Sands and Dent. Sandy and his wife had often visit Grange and they loved the place. His wife, when asked about which station he should choose, said: "Put in for them both." He did so. So he went down to Derby for his examination in commercial and operating matters and an interview which might see him elevated to the rank of Stationmaster.

When the tests were carried out, he was then directed to the office of Mr Rudgard, who in effect presided over the LMS. As a response to a knock on the door, he heard the gruff command: "Come in." He did so, finding that Mr Rudgard was sitting at a huge desk on a raised area of the office. Mr Rudgard was a big man physically as well as in the administrative sense. He had a deep voice to suit his bulk.

"Sit down," he commanded, being sparing with his words. Sandy sat down.

The Chief ran his eyes down the paper which had been put before him. He seemed pleased with what he saw. Then he said: "How would you like to go to Dent?" Sandy replied: "I wouldn't, sir." "What?" demanded the Chief, and Sandy qualified his remark: "But I'll go!" Mr Rudgard said: "It's a bit bleak up there." Sandy replied: "I know it is. I've been up there." The Chief said: "That should stand you in good stead. But you'll not be there for long. It's a starting-off place." And this was, indeed, the case. If a Stationmaster was at Dent three months or six months he must consider himself unlucky.

Sandy was appointed Stationmaster at Dent, Class 5, on June 2, 1938. He took charge on October 26. His annual salary of 200 was augmented by two and a-half per cent to cover call-outs for emergencies, a task he had every other week. For Sunday duties, which then could be frequent, he was allowed five per cent of his salary. "This percentage rose gradually, depending on the number of Sundays worked, though if you were approaching a fairly high percentage, a relief man would be sent to cover for you!"

When he took up his duties, he lodged for a while in a cottage behind the Institute at the bottom of the hill. Here lived the elderly Mr Gornall—"he really looked old"—his daughter and her husband. "Adjoining the cottage was the home of Mr Middleton, who owned a little shop and also ran a taxi. The taxi was well-filled when we organised an evening trip to Morecambe Illuminations, the cost per person being half a crown. Mr Middleton arrived with a carload. I couldn't believe my eyes when the last person to clamber out was Old Mr Gornall. He said: 'I'm going to Morecambe.' I said: 'Be careful'."

When that special train returned, late in the day, Sandy was the only person on duty, having let the staff go home. All but Mr Gornall dis-embarked. He'd been last seen when the train arrived in Morecambe and he'd gone striding off, as bright as you like. "I walked down to his home and told his daughter that father had not returned. She said they had some relatives in Morecambe but she did not think he would have visited them because they lived a fair way from the station. I then made inquiries at Hellifield but no one had seen him get off the train there. On the Monday afternoon, Old Bonnyface (which ran to Hawes and back) arrived and who should get off but Old Mr Gornall. He came off smiling as though he'd had the time of his life. I said: 'Where the devil have you been? We've been worried to death.' He had seen some friends of the family and they had asked him to stay— until Monday morning."

Sandy gently pointed out that he had been on an evening excursion which had cost him the modest sum of half a crown. He would have to charge him the excess fare, which was 7s.6d. "Nay, I've come back," he said. Patiently Sandy said he had to return on the excursion train. He said: "Seven-and-six is a lot o' money." Of course, he was not surcharged. Sandy just could not do it to an old man who had provided him with hospitality. "So I did nothing about it. He went off, chuckling. If they'd known at Head Office what I'd done—or, more to the point, what I hadn't done—they would have been looking for a new Stationmaster . . ."

Getting his possessions from Heysham to Dent had presented the new Stationmaster with no difficulties. They were, of course, consigned by rail, more precisely in a goods wagon, which was lodged in the siding. Sandy travelled on the same train. "It was quite good weather—then! I knew what it could turn to because I'd had some before."

It was the start of a long association with Dentdale, its characterful people and also the wildlife of the area. This Stationmaster would shoot grouse from behind walls and the railway snow-fences. He would fish from Deeside, the old sporting lodge of the Bentincks of Underley Hall, down to Hell's Cauldron, a waterfall situated three-parts of the way between Cowgill and Dent Town. He would visit the Devil's Pulpit, one of innumerable quaint features formed in the bed of the river by the force of acidic water on limestone.

Stationmaster's House

THE HOUSE looks large from the outside, an effect created by its being designed in the shape of a letter T. Because the Midland Railway was aware of the rigours of the weather, they gave the house of their chief emissary at Dent several protective skins. Working from the inside, there were two inches of insulating plaster, then brickwork, which was also a good insulator—two layers of brick with a rubble fill. The outer layer was dressed sandstone, not limestone, as on viaducts, where it was prone to crack.

The Stationmaster's House became noted because it had an early example of double-glazed windows. In fact, they were not of the modern type but simply double windows, fitted about six inches apart. They were fitted to the lounge, living room and an upstairs bedroom. Slates on two sides of the house "kept the weather off", the overlapping slates being set on a framework of wood. Eventually, slates were fitted all round and "stopped the snow from sticking". The slates were beginning to rattle in the gales in the 1940s. Eventually they were removed, the area which they had protected being (unwisely) cement-rendered.

When Cecil and Margaret Sanderson lived here (1938-45), the porch was used as a store for provisions which might be needed in emergency if the snow-dogs began to howl. "Before the bad weather started, I went to Dinsdales in Dent and ordered a bag of flour, a big bag of sugar, potatoes and other things, to see us through the worst of the weather till spring." The produce was transported from Dent Town by Rowland Sanderson, who—as already related—owned a lorry, one of the first motor vehicles to negotiate the steep hill. "Visitors to the Stationmaster's House who lived in towns were amazed when they saw our special foodstore." Beyond the porch, the first room on the right was the living room. A passage led to the kitchen and across the passage from the kitchen was the lounge, or "front room", with its superb fine-weather view of the dale.

Outside the kitchen window was a little yard with a high wall. Now and again it filled with snow. As Sandy explains: "Living at the Stationmaster's House made a person weather-wise. The Dent weather was ferocious. I daren't shave for weeks on end because, if I did, I'd lacerate my face. In Dent conditions, the snow does not fall from above. It's lateral snow, with ice and hailstones mixed in. And it's fierce. If you were not cautious, it would blow you off your feet." The north-east was the snow-quarter. A blizzard would oversweep Widdale Fell and descend on Dent Station, howling like a Dervish. A north-easter would fill one of the big cuttings to the north of Dent Station. "That particular cutting was lined up with my back yard! Early in the morning, I'd open the back door and be confronted by a solid block of snow and ice—right to the top!"

Sandy would spread a large sheet across the kitchen floor and then begin the task of clearing the door space and digging his way across the yard to the water-closet. "It was a proper toilet—not like the old Horton-in-Ribblesdale three-seater!" He then had to make a pathway to the gate, beside the house and into the gill, to draw water from Monkey Beck. In bitter winter weather, the gravity-fed supply froze. So did the water-tub in the yard which collected 'soft' water from the roof of the house to be used on washing day. Water from the beck was transported in buckets to fill the 'copper' and any other suitable containers."

At nightime, Sandy would collect a bucketful of water and throw it over the windows and the front door to seal them to keep out the cold draughts. "If you got a draught in the house, it was like a knife cutting your throat." When looking

THE STATIONMASTER'S HOUSE

for kindling for a fire, it was pointless seeking trees in an area like Dent Station. Coal for the domestic grate was bought from Len Haygarth, to be supplemented by occasional large cobs of coal pushed from a passing train. "The fireman did not particularly want all the trouble of breaking up ultra-big pieces of coal; he would have a huge piece on the footplate, just ready, and then he'd get his shovel behind it and push it on to the side of the line...Trainloads of coal were delivered to various stations on the Settle-Carlisle and sometimes it would wriggle off the top and drop at the side. On a Sunday morning, I'd walk from Dent towards Rise Hill Tunnel with a bucket and fill it with small pieces of coal."

At Dent, wind and rain can form a depressing combination. On an evening when there was a special "do"—whist and dominoes—for the Red Cross at the Cowgill Institute, which stood at the bottom of the hill, Sandy's wife made a meat and potato pie. "The ladies in the area took it in turn to make such pies. And they did not stint them. A Dent pie was made in a baking bowl." Sandy volunteered to carry the warm pie down the hill. Margaret put a towel round the huge pie, so that he would not be burnt as he carried it. It was then swaddled in an old mackintosh. As Sandy bore the pie down the hill, rain was hurled at him by a wind full of spite.

"Suddenly this mac blew off the top, my mac flew open, pulling off every button and I started to burn my hands on the pie dish. I remember water rushing down either side of the Coal Road. I slipped into one of the runnels. My hat was blown away. When I got to the Institute, I was absolutely shattered. The ladies took off my gumboots and fitted me out to make me look respectable. And all that was caused by weather coming from the west!"

Snow imparted a feeling of isolation. In the 1942-43, Sandy decided to walk down to Cowgill. "The gill running past my house was full of snow which had become frozen over to such an extent it would bear my weight. I walked to Cowgill down that gill, following a straight line instead of the curving road. My wife would not believe me when I got back. She said I had not been long. I told her I'd found a short-cut."

The Stationmaster's House was sold by British Railways during the Beeching period of the late 1960s. In 1977, a year after the Settle-Carlisle became a centenarian, the Holmes family of Batley became the proud owners of what had been the Stationmaster's House. Roy and Jenny Holmes took possession on April 1 which (as Jenny observes) was the centenary of the house. The slate roof, set at a very steep

angle, catches the weather. Roy says: "It cost half the purchase price of the house to get the roof fixed. And ten years
later, it needed fixing again." At first the house was used as
a Dales retreat. Then the family "flitted" here from Batley.
Apart from Roy and Jenny there were two children, Ellen and
Ptolemy. During their schooldays they normally travelled to
and from Dent by taxi. In snowtime, it was not unknown for
the children to sledge down the hill to Lea Yeat to catch their
transport at the dale road.

At Dent station, the Holmes family were soon coping with
a west wind which frequently delivers rain uphill. Umbrellas
are useless and (as Jenny says) "there's only me goes to Kendal in wellies and a big coat. The others are trotting round in
their Marks and Sparks suits and high heels." When the
wind blows up here, the roof tiles dance. "You get the feeling
that the whole roof is going to fly off." Roy mentions that
when they bought the property, they were curious about the
iron railing beside the steps leading to the house. Soon they
realised it was to hang on to in a strong wind, to avoid being
blown down the side of the building. When Roy was still
working in Batley and commuting to Dent, there was a wild
day when Jenny rang up and reported: "We've lost the carport." This structure, made of wood and corrugated iron,
was blown away, ending up in the beck-bottom. There was
not a scratch on the car which it had been sheltering.

Roy installed a pumping system to deliver water to a point
above the stair well. "It's quite a good system—though a bit
noisy. We've never been without electricity for more than
three days." The bathroom is on the ground floor, as are the
living room cum kitchen and the front room, the window of
which frames one of the fairest fine-weather views in
England—of verdant Dentdale and its flanking fells. Jenny
finds the near presence of Dent station comforting. She can
hop on a train and within the hour be shopping at Settle.

When a Steam Special is due, Jenny stares with amusement
at the quantity of camera equipment brought along by

enthusiasts to record its progress. "People don't ask if they can stand in our garden—they just come! They'll break anything down to clear a way to get a picture." Two train-photographers fought on the bridge, hitting each other with their cameras. The trouble arose when a latecomer occupied space being used by someone who had been there for ages.

A succession of Stationmasters have responded to the challenge of the wind-blasted, frost-stung plot which serves as a garden. Cecil Sanderson, in the 1930s, selected for cultivation a v-shaped plot across the station approach as a vegetable garden. Drystone walls would shelter the tender plants from the worst of the weather. "I planted all sorts of things and they came through. Full stop! The wind found a way through and blew the plants out of the ground. So I gave it up." The garden is still of the wild variety, with the standard Dales "mix", including moorland plants, tormentil and scabious. In due season there are dog daisies, foxgloves and the purple spires of rosebay willow herb. Jenny says: "For the first few years, we chopped the willow herb down. We realise now that it provides a good show." She planted out some geraniums, which "cried all summer and never flowered. When I brought them indoors, they were so big they looked like cabbages." She then planted some "salad stuff", which appealed to the rabbits. Jenny soon realised that an exposed, train spotter-trampled location 1,150 ft above seal level needs some robust local plants. "There's no point in doing anything else than nature intended—and it's pretty."

Wildlife is at home here. Sandy remembers when there was an invasion of grouse from the moor above. Mr Braithwaite, an ex-Lord Mayor of Leeds, moved from his home in the Leeds area in the late 1930s, as war-clouds gathered. He had bought Whernside Manor, in Dentdale. Mr Braithwaite's son was Major A N Braithwaite, who was the MP for the Buckrose Division of East Yorkshire. Some of the top men of the government—Harold Macmillan and Duncan Sandys among them—would arrive by train for the grouse-shooting and were accommodated at Whernside Manor. They invariably sat in the station office when arriving or departing, having a chat with Sandy.

"The gamekeeper would tip me off when shooting was to take place on a particular moor. Grouse, once they are driven off their home moor, are lost and they go haywire. They fly in all directions, as though they have no control over where they are going. So I used to go behind the snow-screens above Dent station and shoot birds as they came over."

This skyline garden is a landing strip for a pheasant from the moor-edge, a bird which is in raucous voice at 5 a.m. Says Jenny Holmes: "It drove us mad with its crowing when it was doing its courting." The space under the eaves of the house holds a row of clay nests belonging to house martins.

The Permanent Way

In frosty weather, the trackbed on Arten Gill viaduct used to lift. By heck, you hadn't got to go so fast over it 'cos it was like driving over a corrugated roof.

A Skipton driver, c1950.

BRUTE force as well as skill were needed for re-laying track in the days when a length was sixty yards and, on a Sunday, as many as 150 men attended to three quarters of a mile at a time. The new wooden sleepers had previously been laid beside the track and men on piece rates bored holes with augurs, putting on the chairs, placing a spike in one hole and a plug in the other. "Nippers" tarred the plugs and spikes for durability. For the re-laying, all the platelayers between Skipton and Hawes were out. The job had been broken down into various tasks, each given to a gang, so that work proceeded quickly and smoothly.

One Sunday, while re-laying at Dent Head, a lengthman named Frank had a new sixty-foot rail tipped on to his foot. "He was assisted to the nearby cabin. Sinbad, one of his fellow workers, elected to treat him and, with another, got one boot off, amidst groans and curses. Frank carefully removed the affected stocking, up-ended it, and shook it vigorously over a piece of newspaper in case there had been an involuntary amputation. However, all was fairly straightforward. We had salvolatile to use in place of iodine. I shudder to think what the reaction from Frank would have been if faced with iodine."

Willie Slinger, a very conscientious ganger at Garsdale, when carrying out his Sunday morning examination, also marked out such defects that he saw. "In the afternoon, he and his wife, with the lever pole, heel, shovel and beater, 'tamped' the worst depressions. Willie tamped while his wife operated the lever.'' One of the many Ivisons applied for a sub-ganger's position. The Examiner came to a question about rail-creep and tight joints. He said to Tom: ''Tell me what you know about rail-creeps and tight joints.'' Tom allowed a few seconds for thought co-ordination and then he simplied the whole complex problem by saying: ''T'b...s grows.''

Dick, who worked in the Slip and Drainage gang in the summer of 1932, recalled that the gang consisted of a ganger and eight men. Dick lodged with a couple and their four children, so the place was cramped. ''If you wanted a bath, you used a tin bath in the wash-house or went in the river. It was a grand big wash-house. To warm the water up, you pinched a spare sleeper off the railway and cut it up for fuel.''

In wet weather, men sat in the cabins—one cabin per length and another near each large viaduct or tunnel. Many of these lengthmen's cabins were not of standard issue but erected by the gangs before the 1914-18 war. Sleepers were used for the walls but there might be a slate roof. There was a saying on the line: ''During fog or falling snow, into the cabin you must go.'' Coal for the fire was normally delivered, but if supplies were low, or some better coal was wanted, a platelayer attracted the attention of a passing footplate crew, who threw off some cobs.

The fireplace had a metal top on which food could be cooked or kept warm. The gangers needed something substantial, such as ''half a collop of bacon and a couple of eggs.'' Forms stood round the room and there was also a table. The stone cabins erected for snow-clearers at Dent were useful at any time if the weather was inclement.

At Dent and Garsdale, getting soaked was a common experience. On a day of torrential rain, Old Adam went into a cabin at the end of Garsdale platform and, being wet to the skin, he stripped off. ''I just put a damn great fire on, and hung my clothes before t'fire. I must have fell asleep. When I woke up, it was dinnertime. I got my clothes on and then I couldn't get out of t'cabin. It was that bloody hot, I couldn't lift t'sneck!''

Cecil Sanderson recalls when he and his wife might have a Sunday walk by the track down to Stone House, Arten Gill, where lived Bill Bannister, a Leeds man who arrived at Dent as signalman, and Nellie, his wife, who was daughter of a local farmer. ''In the summertime, it was a lovely walk; there was such a nice view of the whole valley. We would probably have tea there. And vice versa; they would come up to our place. When we'd been to the Bannisters house, we would climb up the steep bank on to the line near Arten Gill viaduct. Sometimes it would start to rain. We'd find a cabin and, if it was locked up, I had an idea where the key would be. I'd open the place up and go inside. It was always lovely and warm in a cabin.''

The ganger ''looked the length'' each morning. Meanwhile, his men sat in the cabin. ''They'd be nice and dry; he'd be getting wet through if it was raining.'' Some huts on the Settle-Carlisle were known by the names of gangers—Adam's Cabin, Tom's Cabin, Ted's Cabin. (Ted and Tom were brothers). One shack became known as Gangster's Cabin for when rain fell, the assembled men smoked black twist or played cards—usually nap—for pennies. ''The atmosphere was generally pretty thick.''

The cabins occupied by the platelayers in wet spells or at meal-times were the most homely little places you ever saw, ''all seasoned and homely and always aired.'' The platelayers were far-seeing and, giving early thought to where they would be working next, arranged that someone would light a fire in advance to ensure the cabin was not damp. ''Some cabins were made of stone, but the majority were of sleepers with good hard wooden tops covered with thick felt which was kept tarred. In some cases, tar had been applied so thickly and so often it used to run on a hot day.''

The interior of a cabin was always limewashed for brightness and hygene. The most conspicuous feature was an iron stove, which was square, with a little flap in the front. "They'd put a kettle on t'top and a pie in the oven. Then t'platelayers would sit round the hot stove and spit in the fire." On winter mornings, platelayers did not turn out for work until it was properly light and they were back at the cabin by 3-30 on the shortest days. They did not work in the rain. "If it was chucking it down, they slunk about in t'cabin all day...Heat was vital. When platelayers moved into another area for a spell of work there was always someone at the cabin early to get the fire going."

They did some work, of course! In bad weather, the points were kept clear by the ganger and platelayers. They used salt, though in the event of this melting ice and turning to water it might soon be dispersed and the situation reverted to what it was before the salt had been used. Sandy relates that during his term at Dent station, experiments were being carried out—unsuccessfully—with the steam-clearing of the points. For a while, it worked. Then it iced over and the points were impeded.

When rails became slippery—though in those days, unlike today, the trains were heavy and frequent and leaves jettisoned in autumn were not a problem—the driver would open sand-boxes on his locomotive, the sand trickling down on to the driving wheels and subsequently on to the rails.

In the Signal Box

SETTLE-CARLISLE men were resourceful. When Billy Stansfield died in the box at Dent Head, the Stationmaster, Jack Sheard, took over the box until someone else could be summoned. Up to the late 1930s, all boxes had telegraph instruments. At Dent, the signalman could receive and despatch postal telegrams, the company providing a bicycle so that telegrams might be delivered by the porter. The Dent call was RH.

The best known of the Dent signalman, Jack Sedgwick, was fond of saying: "T'owd place has most certainly known better days." He remained chirpy to the last. I can see him now, his face creased in a smile, his eyes bright, a cloth cap worn well back on the head and a wisp of smoke rising from his pipe.

A signalman was expected to wear a collar and tie. "We kept these in a locker—till an inspector was seen. Then we soon slipped 'em on." When Eric Treacy, "the Railway Bishop", visited Dent at first, Jack and his friends had no idea of his high church position, for Treacy wore an ordinary tie. "Aye" recalled Jack, "he used to say he enjoyed listening to Dent box talk afore the men fun out he was a parson." Incidentally, a local man, Jim Harper, died when on duty at Dent box.

Cecil Sanderson has many happy memories of Jack Sedgwick. "When he was on two to ten duty at Dent box, he would walk up the gill, tickling trout. He knew where they were—tucked in holes at the side of the beck. Sometimes he'd call at the house and say to my wife: "Would you like a bit o' fish for tea?' She would—this being a time of food rationing. Jack liked a few trout. He'd fry them up on the stove in his signal box."

It grieved Jack that when the box was made redundant, the woodwork was put to the torch. It had been his workplace for many years. He was a conscientious man who, none the less, did a bit of haircutting in the box. A photograph showing him at work on a lile lad with a good crop of hair was to be seen, not published, in case the railway authority took umbridge. I am sure that this was one of many a paying pastime to take place in a Settle-Carlisle signal box.

Jack told me that electricity for working the box originally came from batteries, firstly the wet variety, then dry batteries. These were maintained by men who travelled up from Settle. The signals at Dent had frequently to be cut out of snow drifts. The "distant" was in such a bad condition that after the 1947 storm an inter-distant signal was provided. When a driver saw this off, he could put steam on to surge through Dent Cutting.

Sandy was intrigued by the aforementioned trout-tickling; "I used to see him coming but wondered why his head should occasionally go out of sight. He was putting his hands under the boulders at the side of the gill and picking out trout mesmerised by the 'tickling' process. It never worked for me. I couldn't get hold of the damn things; they wriggled out of my hand. I think they knew Jack!"

Bill Bannister, who started his railway career as a porter at Leeds and became a porter at Dent, qualified as a signalman and worked in the Dent box for over thirty years. Bill was a devoted servant of the Settle-Carlisle. The railway might not provide him with a fortune but it had given him steady employment when, after the first world war, he had begun to put his life together again. It had also seen him through the Depression years of the late 1920s and 1930s. As his son, Brian, observes: "He had a job and he was grateful for it. He was typical of those conscientious men whose lives revolved around the railway." Having been through grim events in the war, Bill Bannister had not a lot of time for trivia. "He was very black and white—a thing was either right or wrong.

There was no grey area.''

Bill Bannister organised his life to the second. As a smoker of cigarettes who rolled his own, he prepared nine for every shift. The first cigarette was smoked as he began his vigil in the Dent box. The others were smoked at hourly intervals. In those thirty-odd years of walking from Stone House, up Arten Gill, on to the railway and along the two mile stretch to the station, he was late only twice—once when, going over the stile at the top of Arten Gill, he broke his ankle, and the other time when he awoke to find a beam adjacent to the house chimney was smouldering. ''He didn't miss work—he was just late on those two occasions.''

Brian occasionally visited him at the signal box, but he did not encourage this. It might deflect him from his work. ''I was in the signal box many times with some of his colleagues. He and Jackie Sedgwick worked together for donkey's years.

Above—Jack Sedgwick, Dent signalman. *Right*—the Dent box, which was demolished.

I've had my hair cut by Jackie and one or two of the others."
Bill Bannister's hobby was the repairing of wireless sets—the
old type of set, with valves. "Once transisters came in, he
gave it up." His son recalls when Bill heated up a huge
soldering iron in the fire—"we had no electricity then"—and
solder really intricate things with it. "I think he was one of
the first people up the dale who had a cat's whiskers set. As
a boy at Stone House, I remember when a chap came over
from Hawes once a week bringing a supply of wet batteries
for hire." Stone House had proper aerials. "If the weather
became thunderly, you threw a switch just inside the window. Then, if the aerial was struck by lightning, it would be
earthed."

The signal box at Dent Head was small, with three signals
each way and a cross-over road. Mr Sanderson, who
operated here for a short time in 1934, recalls that the duty
man reached the box by field footpath from the road. "Some
of the men who worked there came from Ribblehead via Blea
Moor and, if they were pushed, actually through Blea Moor
Tunnel, which could be a dangerous experience. Others
walked or cycled in from Dent or Cowgill. It was a draughty
box, not far from a viaduct and deep cutting."

During a thunderstorm in the 1930s the signalman saw a
"thunderbolt" fall at the door of the platelayer's cabin on the
up-line side, quite near the box. In the signal box, a blue
flame or light seemed to run the length of the instrument
shelf. There was a faint jingle of bells and also a smell of
sulphur. "I ran across to the cabin. All four PW men were
under the seats, rather shocked but otherwise quite well. I
returned to the signal box to find that most of the instruments
were affected. The dog teeth of the arresters on the phone
connections were blackened."

By 1984, the signal box still stood but the signals had gone.
All that remained was a white panel (a back plate for a
semaphore) on the overbridge serving the Coal Road.

Hearing the telephone ring at Dent recently, I lifted the

receiver and found myself talking to the signalman at Blea Moor, the most famous of the Settle-Carlisle boxes because of its remote situation. Here worked George Horner, who has also achieved celebrity status as a raconteur with a seemingly inexhaustible supply of Settle-Carlisle stories. He was previously at Ribblehead. His first experience of working Blea Moor was as a summer relief in 1953. ''I remember t'date because that summer the express piled up there. It happened in the afternoon and I was t'night man.'' George's father was one of the elite group of Blea Moor signalmen. Just when George joined the group, he found it hard to recall, ''I've

A QUICK HAIRCUT

been flittin' about that much...it was in the late 50s.''
George had worked on almost all the boxes on the Drag. He
had ''relieve'' at Garsdale and recalled the famous Turntable
as it was in his heyday. ''They ran on to it with t'engine and
then they used to shove the turntable round by hand.''

George and his father were at Blea Moor in the transition
period, when steam was being phased out and diesel traction
introduced. ''You had to go against convention and decide
which was fastest and should have the 'road'. You didn't
always go by class. You'd ask t'bloke behind: 'What's this
divvil got on? Is he a steamer or a diesel'?'' There were
teething troubles with diesels when they were brought into
service on the Settle-Carlisle. George says: ''The thing about
an old steamer was that it might not do ower well at times,
especially when it had some bad coal or summat like that, but
it always managed to twine itself to t'next signal box so that
they could get at 'im. In t'early days, if a diesel decided to lay
doon, it lay doon where it was! And you'd lost 'im!''

When the author first knew Blea Moor there was a lively
railway community here, living in several houses. The
original box stood beside the down-line. The new box, on its
brick base, beside the up-line, dates from late LMS times.
George explains: ''The levers of t'present box are closer-set
than t'old ones. It's a left hand frame with 30 levers. You are
facing t'back wall instead of looking through t'front window.'' For the night shift, George had to be at Blea Moor at
10 p.m. ''Unless it was a brilliant moonlit night—which, of
course, you did get from time to time—you needed a torch.
If you were on from 2 till 10, you'd see your mate coming to
relieve you. You'd notice his leet coming over t'hill.''

Blea Moor being a newish box, it had more modern toilet
facilities than those at the old signal boxes, where—says
George—''a lile tin shack stood a few yards from t'signal.
That sort of toilet wasn't always safe in a real strong wind!
I've heard of one tekkin' off wi' a fellow sat theer!'' Blea
Moor's was an Elsan, at the top of the steps. ''It was cleaned

out every week to see it was kept decent. It was so handy. You just went out t'door and turned to t'right—and there it was!'' It is related that a pipe-smoking signalman, sitting in state, kindling his pipe, dropped the match between his legs into the pan. After a while, he was conscious of getting warm. The match had not been properly blown out and had ignited the chemicals in the pan.

When George went to Blea Moor, the signal box shared a water supply with the houses. ''It had a tap at t'bottom of t'steps. The supply used to get bunged up from time to time. Old Jack Dawson, who was ganger in t'Tunnel, was told that t'watter was petering out and would say in a slow, calm voice: 'I'll go and see to it'. And he did. Next thing you knew, t'watter supply was resumed.'' Lighting was by courtesy of a paraffin lamp. ''After a bit, we got hanging Aladdin lamps. Then we got quite modern. They gave us Tilly lamps.''

To the box came the locomen who were waiting to change to a new train. Platelayers wanting a brew at dinnertime arrived at the door. Now and again Eric Treacy, who had been taking photographs and was now chilled to be marrow, was given a cup of tea. George and his Dad provided lots of cups of tea. ''We didn't just take a day's supply. We took a packet of tea at a time and shoved it into a jar. We used it till it were done.''

I asked George about sheep. Animals strayed on to the railway looking for a toothsome bite of grass on the banks. Sometimes, taken by surprise at the sudden appearance of a fast train, they were knocked down and killed. But mainly, they avoided death. George told me that ''a lot of 'em were lambed on t'railway side. They were brought up there. It was their real home!'' George related that a platelayer who came from Hawes did his best to keep the sheep away. When he was half a mile away, you could hear him shouting at the sheep. ''His language wasn't always that patent. He landed at Blea Moor one day. I said: 'There's an owd devil that's bin on t'engineer's sidings all morning. Get her off!' His language started to flow. Baa-sheep went ower t'hill and down into t'bottom and ower t'wall and into beck. Yon platelayer was pleased wi' himself. He came back into middle of t'track wi' his spanner to tighten a bolt up in crossover road. All of a sudden he heard: "Baaa'. T'owd devil was back and stamping his feet at him. It was ten minutes afore I stopped laughin'.''

A signalman on the Long Drag became an authority on Hot Axle Boxes. One of the brethren explained this to me. ''A wheel was solid on its axle; the whole lot turned. An axle box was in two halves, fastened up wi' bolts. If you got a divided box, where a bolt came loose and t'bottom half dropped away, that was the half that had the oily pad in. It then overheated. It would get so hot it would strike fire. You'd see it blazing. When a box burnt out, you got a 'squealer'. You'd hear it. Now and again, if you went to t'door as a train was going by, you could even smell it.'' A neglected Hot Axle Box soon led to the vehicle dropping on to the wheel. It was then out of action.

The White Stuff

EVERYONE has his winter memory of Dent. "T'first and last flakes o' snow allus seem to land up here." The Midland had confidently followed the example of the Highland Railway and erected snow fences at the most exposed stretches. They were just sleepers on end, with fencing wire to hold them up. Little maintenance was carried out. Periodically, an inspector signed a form to confirm they were still in existence. He supposed that the railway was still paying rent on the land they occupied. But the snow fences were next to useless in the full fury of a Pennine blizzard.

Cecil Sanderson (Sandy), who took up his duties as Stationmaster in the autumn of 1938, was soon aware of the ferocity of a Dent blizzard. The troublesome quarter was the North East, and the snow overswept Widdale Fell to be arrested (briefly) by the snow fences, which did not mean much. "Snow was heaped up behind the first row. In no time at all, snow would be over the top and into the next row. It would go into the third row. The next thing was the up-waiting room, then the up-line. I've seen snow piled up so that the top of the drift went from the roof of the waiting room straight across to the door of my office on the other platform. We used to get drifts up to forty foot deep in the big cutting between Dent and Rise Hill. And a train—even a snow plough—might be buried in it."

He adds: "I used to get my information about the weather from the Stationmaster at Ribblehead, who prepared a summary every hour for forwarding to the Met Office. He used to send up these balloons to assess the height of the clouds. He also collected information about the temperature and so forth. A report from Ribblehead, supplemented by local signs, such as that of farmers gathering sheep and moving them down the fellside, indicated snow in the offing, I'd tell Skipton Control, with a recommendation that snow ploughs should be mustered. They were promptly sent from Skipton to Dent and were put in the sidings.''

Sometimes the drifts in the cuttings would be twenty feet deep, which resulted in the up-line being written off for traffic. Concentration was focussed on the down-line which was the only track available for all traffic. The system was now ''single-line working by pilotman'', who was in charge of movements of all traffic in conjunction with the Controls at Carlisle and Skipton Offices. Sandy cannot remember the line coming to a complete standstill except perhaps for half an hour. ''To me, that was a miracle. The conditions were to be seen to be believed.'' Two locomotives, back to back, each with a plough, enabled clearing to take place in either direction. Sometimes there was a vehicle, a van, in between two locomotives with ploughs. The van was intended to accommodate men with shovels. It often caused the outfit to become too flexible, resulting in a derailment.

With single-line working, the object (says Sandy) was to have as much traffic as possible as close as possible. ''I was the pilotman on the snow-ploughs. I would get through to Control and get to know what trains were coming up from Skipton. We would arrange to get as many trains as we could, moving as close together as we good, bearing in mind the necessity for the system to remain safe. When I got a train signalled as coming past Ribblehead, I set off from Dent to Garsdale over the single line—if that was the extent of the single-line—or, if it was further, to Kirkby Stephen.'' This shows the need for a small box like Dent Head to be among the larger boxes, making such an operation possible without having two trains in one section.

The idea was to hit a drift of snow as hard as possible. Two Class 8 engines represented nearly 200 tons so the snow was inclined to be pushed well away from the line and cleared a path, which was the object of the operation. Sandy has been "half way up to the neck" in snow. The Hawes line was prone to be overblown with snow and was ploughed out whenever possible.

The permanent way men bore the brunt of the effort to clear snow. "I remember the big snows well. You'd to walk

Wintry Topics

S & C man: "Tha'll not get much snow down 'ere then?" Furness man: "Oh, we get a fair lot. I've seen it cover t'rails." S & C man: "Cover t'rails? I've seen it cover t'b....y engines."
T G Flinders, The Settle-Carlisle route Re-visited (1985).

Around Dent and Garsdale, there was that much snow, you didn't know where to put it.
A ganger (recalling 1947).

It was here, during the extraordinary winter of 1946-7, that Hubert Foster went to take photographs of the snow blocks—photographs that went before the Cabinet and revealed more than reams of written report the extent to which Nature had seized in a strangehold some of the greatest arteries of the nation's transport.
O S Nock and Eric Treacy,
Main Lines Across the Borders (1960).

As soon as you couldn't see a rail, you wanted the snow plough out. It didn't always work like that. Very often you'd ring up from Skipton and somebody in Carlisle would say: It isn't snowing here." Can you think of a dafter answer?
Permanent Way Man, 1963.

over t'top of t'bridges. I once walked up the roof of the waiting room at Dent—and didn't know it was there till later." The most memorable winter was 1947, when Old Charlie of Dent—a conscientious ganger—could not leave the house. Snow was piled up outside the front and back doors. So he asked his wife to empty the pantry, which she did. He dug into the drift at the back of the house and got rid of the snow by piling it up in the pantry. Charlie then squeezed his way into the yard and went to work.

Famous snow winters which are well remembered at Dent include 1942, 1947 and 1962. Flakes of the hard-wearing type swept in from the north-east. (Snow from the west is usually sloppy and thaws by teatime).

Dent's snow defences—the aforementioned rows of upreared sleepers—are useless when the snow outstays its welcome. "They thought the fencing would make the snow accumulate short of the railway," Jack Sedgwick (signalman) once told me. He added: "It didn't stay off the lines. It just carried on regardless." In 1947, the Dent length was blocked for eight weeks and, when they'd warmed up, the snow-cutters were able to hang their coats on the tops of the telegraph poles. "The wind causes the mischief. In that bad winter, it blew day and night."

Best remembered at Dent are the blizzards of February and March, 1947, which blocked the line for eight weeks. Dent is in the tract of countryside terrorised by the Helm Wind, a turbulence created when air from the east, cooled in its climb to the edge of the Pennine escarpment, in the vicinity of High Cup Nick, pours over like a waterfall and meets the comparatively warm air of the Eden Valley. The snowfall may be moderate but the remorseless wind, blowing for days on end, sweeps it off the open fells into railway cuttings. In 1947, snow was piled to the height of the overbridges.

The answer by the railway company was to have specially adapted locomotives fitted with steel ploughs, one on each locomotive so that the unit could plough backwards or forwards with equal felicity. A number of goods brake vans were made available as communication centres, also messes and dormitories for weary men. Providentially, in the autumn, Dent had been given extra facilities—a depot including accommodation for ten men, who might eat and sleep here; and a supply of coal.

IN 1947, THE DENT LENGTH WAS BLOCKED FOR EIGHT WEEKS

During the 1947 blockage, a jet engine obtained from Rolls Royce at Barnoldswick was placed on a flat wagon and sent up the Drag. The theory was that it would blow snow off the tracks. Alas, the snow was packed too hard. "Yon engine buzzed away for I don't know how long; it managed to clear a yard o' snow. So they gave it up as a bad job..."

At Dent in 1947, cornices of snow overhung the track. It was decided to blast them away. Like the jet engine idea, the scheme was useless. A permanent way man recalled: "All tha could see was a puff o' black smoke. T'snow was hardly disturbed." When one of the Dent cuttings had to be cleared, railborne snow-ploughs were summoned. A plough-train of the 1940s consisted of two locomotives of the 0-6-0 type, with a plough at either end. "That was in case it got stuck."

Footplate men, flimsily protected by tarpaulin sheets over the cab and by the side blinds, braced themselves as a plough dashed towards a four-foot deep barrier of snow. "It was terrifying, especially in daylight. As the snow got deeper, you could hear it scratching on the engine." Then the snow came in, between the floorboards of the cab, into every nook and cranny. It squeezed in, just like toothpaste from a tube. "Snow could be packed so hard, the engine became belly-bound. Wheels began to spin. And all the time you could be standing on t'footplate up to your waist in snow."

In the winter of 1962-3, both lines were blocked towards the end of January. Conditions became impossible on the 20th, after the 10.5 p.m. Edinburgh to St Pancras sleeping car express had been allowed through. The valiant snow-ploughers had been working non-stop, but the train became stranded near Dent, a terrifying experience for the passengers considering it was 3 a.m. and the carriages were being rocked by a bitterly cold wind. The spirited railwaymen actually got the passengers back to Carlisle in the last three coaches, snow ploughs opening up a way for a rescue locomotive which ran to Garsdale, where the locomotive from an abandoned freight train bore them back to safety.

I recall the inconvenience of having the Settle-Carlisle blocked. At that time I was living in Settle and had an appointment in Edinburgh, which normally would have been a simple journey. With the Drag closed, I motored to Hellifield, travelled via Carnforth, with the train scraping drifts, and took the Lancaster-Carlisle. The direct route to Edinburgh being blocked by snow, I journeyed to Glasgow, from where I crossed to Edinburgh. Next morning, with all lines blocked but the East Coast route, I returned to Hellifield via York and Leeds. I cannot recall seeing sleepers—just two shiny rails protruding above snow. The only visible greenery was by the Solway on the outward journey. (The Settle-Carlisle was blocked for five days).

In that desperate winter, some ploughs being used were

made of wood, sheathed with metal. "They brought in the big engines, Class 8s, whenever they could. You wanted a loco of about ninety tons," said Isaac Hailwood, of Hellifield, one of the unsung heroes of Dent Cutting. Isaac, who had worked his way up to driver, loved his camera but rarely used it. We were fellow members of the local photographic class. Only rarely did I see any "snaps" he had taken. In 1963, with his engine on duty at Dent, Isaac Hailwood operated his camera in conditions which few people have seen. That was the winter when—to quote Isaac—"all you could see of Dent station was one big block of snow."

MAROONED IN SHALE CUTTING

Cornices reared elegantly but dangerously over twenty foot drifts at the edge of the cutting. On his photographs, a faint mark indicated the line of the platform on what was otherwise a gleaming snow cliff. Snow removed from a cutting was transported by goods wagons to Arten Gill viaduct, to be shovelled over the parapets. "We did quite well till t'wind got up." Isaac found beauty in unexpected places: "I'll never forget how lovely it was to see snow falling through the air, in bright sunshine, for over a hundred feet."

It is related that one young soldier, a small chap, was caught by the wind, which lifted him off the wagon. He managed to put a foot on the parapet wall and dropped between the wall and the wagon. "Yon lad could easily have been blown over and fallen about a hundred feet. He was in a terrible state of shock, screaming and blubbering. I went under the wagon, picked him up and gave him a slap across the face. I shook him and told him to go and get his bloody shovel. It had gone flying over the viaduct. He went. He came back, half an hour later, and said he was OK. He'd calmed down."

No regular trains passed through Dent station for five days. The last train to attempt a passage was the sleeping car express between Edinburgh and London, which was encased in snow. Part of the train was removed, with difficulty, and sent northwards with its chilled passengers.

A train was buried in the Shale Cutting. A ganger recalled: "When we were walking that way on a snow-clearing job, one chap fell through the locomotive roof-light. The driver had left it open. It was quite funny, really. But we wondered where the hell he'd gone!"

A large stone cabin near the signal box at Dent, a cabin for the use of snow-clearers during their rest periods, was the one grandly known as Dent Hotel. When the snow ploughs were called out, provisions were despatched to the cabin. Apart from sandwiches, there were nourishing drinks—Oxo, Bovril, tea, coffee. "In fact, anything to bring anybody round if they got cold... The accommodation was rough—but it was a case of 'any port in a storm'. As long as there was a big fire, and plenty o' chaps to get a brew, it was all right. You were theer to do a job, not sit in a cabin!" Another man remembers the "absolute steam" which came off the soaked clothing of a large number of men when they packed themselves into a

cabin. "It was terrible." Sandy recalls that the Dent Hotel
was furnished with "a great long trestle table and a form or
two round the sides. That was it! But it was heaven on earth
to the people who wanted to use it."

Sandy will never forget the night his son was born at Dent
Station House if only because a blizzard was raging. It was
the winter of 1941-2. My son was due to be born round about
the 24th or 25th of the month. I contacted my doctor, who
was at Hawes, and he said I should arrange for a nurse to be
present. He had a friend who was a doctor at Settle who had
friends coming up from London. One of them, Helen
Singleton, was a nurse. She turned out to be the daughter of
Lord Justice Singleton in London. She was told about my
predicament and came up to see my wife. Sandy told her:
"It's not as lovely as you think it is, you know." She thought
the setting was wonderful.

She stayed at the Station House. On the night of my son's
birth, I had to ring the doctor. The nurse was sure the child
would be born that night. And I was on single-line working
between Ribblehead and Kirkby Stephen. I said to Dr Hughes
I would get the snow-plough down to Hawes and bring him
back to Dent. I arranged this with the Control Office. They
agreed, but did not think he would get through. I couldn't
get through. My ploughs would have stuck fast anyway. It
was very bad down the Hawes line." When Sandy rang Dr
Hughes, the doctor said he would come round by road,
following the snow-ploughs. In those days, they had horses
and wooden ploughs. The doctor would have to go to the
Stationmaster's House via Garsdale, Dent and Cowgill. And
then he had to climb a 600 ft hill.

On the railway, a blockage was reported at Aisgill and
single-line working was extended from Garsdale to Kirkby
Stephen. Neither the Stationmaster at Kirkby Stephen or
Garsdale was available, so Sandy was left with extended
single-line operations, which varied with the vagaries of the
weather. "I got to Kirkby Stephen only to be greeted by

some bad news from the signalman. Although I had been on to Control at Carlisle and requested that no expresses should be allowed through, one had indeed been given clearance. Happily, when it arrived at Kirkby Stephen it had only four coaches, as opposed to eight or ten.

Sandy arranged for the ploughs to run through and back on the section including the north side of Aisgill, where a large snow drift had accumulated. This was done with some effort. Sandy had a word with the driver of the express and told him that single-line working extended to Ribblehead. The driver said: "Hell...Give us the road." Sandy mentioned the struggle he had with the snow ploughs. How could he cope with an express train? The driver repeated his request to "give me the road", adding that he would get through.

Sandy now recognised the man who was so sure of his ability to beat the drifts and remarked: "It's never Jack Heseltine, is it?" It was. The two men had known each other at Leeds. Sandy related the story of how his wife was in labour and he was anxious to be at her side. The driver said: "I wish some o' those controllers would spend a night or two up here when t'weather's rough...Give me the road." Sandy mentioned the snowdrift, adding: "It's a bad one." Said the driver: "I'll get you back."

When the drift was in sight, he went straight for it, but the locomotive started to slip—*ya-yaya-yo-yoyo.* The driver asked to be allowed to run back. Sandy said: "Be careful. There are points back there." He knew where they were and he wanted space to run at the drift. He was using the down-line and on the incline between Mallerstang and Aisgill. He ran at the wall of snow. The engine again slipped to a halt—*grrr-rerrr-rowww.* He set back again and made himself a little space and had another run.

Sandy recounted: "He forced his way through that drift and kept the train moving. And he got me back to Dent station. The doctor had walked behind the ploughs all the way to Cowgill and when he got up the hill to my house he was shattered. I found I had a son. He had a rough birth. Margaret and I had him christened (at Cowgill Church) John Duncan Sanderson.''

In the same period, an enormous snow drift formed against a steep bank near the north portal of Blea Moor Tunnel. Sandy, anxious to shorten the single-line working on the up-line by clearing it out, took the ploughs from Dent, swept away two drifts near the snow-fences and reckoned that if they got up some speed over Dent Head viaduct to Blea Moor tunnel, they would shift the big drift.

''We went down this hill to Dent Head. When we passed Arten Gill, I heard a rattle and scratching and the sound of things flying about. A telegraph pole had fallen and the ploughs had smashed it up. We made such jerky progress to Dent Head viaduct, I thought we'd come off the road. And we were approaching a bend. On the other side of the viaduct, we went sailing through the big drift, even though it was deep and frozen. The look-out windows on the cab were smashed and snow came through the holes like sausages. In no time at all, I was knee-deep in snow.

''We entered Blea Moor Tunnel. I asked the driver about the bumping experience at Dent Head viaduct. He had no idea what caused it. Then we heard a tremendous crash on the funnel at the front of the engine. There was a rattling sound across our cab and on to the next engine. I looked out. By the light from the firebox, I saw what appeared to be glass flying about all over the place. I stopped the engine, walked back and there were the remains of an icicle which had formed in one of the air shafts and was as thick as my body.'' The line was again blocked. In January, an Edinburgh-London express was stranded here for five days.

Jack Sedgwick was fond of recalling a snowy night ''when a train got fast and they sent hay from Hellifield. No one wanted to go out and feed the cows, so in the end Bert Nunn, the Loco Inspector from Leeds, and me, made the engine safe and then fed the cows.''

Garsdale Troughs

Them watter-troughs at Garsd'l were hitty-missy.

A Leeds driver.

JUST north of Rise Hill tunnel were the famous Garsdale water-troughs, their fame resting on the fact that they were the highest-situated in the world. The driver of a steam train hoped to replenish his tender and, after watching for signs of their approach, would suddenly say to his firemen: "Gerrit in". The scoop was lowered. "You had your eye on the water gauge, which was in front of you. As soon as it showed about three-quarters full, you started pulling the scoop out. I wanted to see it filled right up to the top, but if the tank overflowed, the fireman was "in lumber". He just couldn't win! A concrete post with an oil lamp was supposed to be the marker for the troughs at night. "Being an oil lamp, it had usually gone out. So on a pitch-black night, you counted bridges. One. Two. At the third bridge, the scoop must go in. If you were in an engine which followed close behind another train which needed water, the trough would still be filling up wi' watter."

The troughs were nearly half a mile in length, being shallow at each end and about six inches deep in the middle. "The train lowered its scoop and lifted it up when the tank had filled. If the scoop was lowered too early, it might catch on the sleepers. It took ten minutes for the water level to build up again. In winter, water which spilled out would freeze, yet water in the trough never seemed to ice over. There was always a lot of traffic to keep it clear.

Formerly, the water was heated by a steam pipe, from a boiler in the tank house. A man stayed there all night stoking up the fire. Water came from a reservoir about half a mile away up the hillside. "We had to go up periodically and clean it out. It was a pleasant enough job, and we might catch a few trout if we let all the water off. We cleaned out the gravel and muck with shovels."

In winter, we spent a lot of time picking ice from between trough and rail. The ice had to be kept below rail level or there could be a train off the road. We had a cabin with a firespot where we could have our meals. There was always plenty of coal which washed off the engines using the troughs. If the tank was overful, then water poured out and washed cobs of coal off the tender. It could be a dangerous job. An overflowing tank lifted the lid and often threw it off. Lids were supposed to be chained down, but sometimes there was no chain. The lids went everywhere.

Among the freight engines stabled at Skipton were "the old Derby 4s". Each had a small tank, "and if you had a heavy load, you'd leave Skipton with a full tank and hope to get some more water at Settle, which should then take you to Blea Moor. After that, you thought of the troughs at Garsdale. If a driver was in a locomotive which had followed close behind another train, the trough would still be filling up with water. "Sometimes it was frozen up and we had to make a water-stop at Appleby. "In times of hard frost, men were sent up to Garsdale troughs to keep them free of ice. A heating system was in operation. The workers slept in the platelayers' cabin and took provisions. Jimmy Antell and Bob Lund were on that job for weeks on end."

As related, it was possible to get too much water, with messy consequences. "Many a time, you'd be getting a tank full before you got half way along a trough. Then water was splashing all over the place. If it was on a passenger train, in warm weather, and some passengers had their windows lowered, they got wet. It was the guard's duty to walk down the train and advise them to shut the windows."

The Tunnel Gang

ONE of the old stories of the Settle-Carlisle country relates to a farm labourer from further up the Dales who found employment with a Dentdale farmer. On the first day, the lad confessed he had never seen a train. The farmer told him to climb up to within sight of the north portal of Blea Moor and stay there till he'd seen a train pass. When the lad returned, he excitedly reported that the train was "freightened of me...When it spotted me, it let out a low moan and buried itself in t'ground."

Blea Moor tunnel was driven for 2,629 yards at a maximum depth of about 500 feet below moor level. The air shafts were impressively deep. Parker Thompson, who was in charge of a party of masons, fancied he would like to have the experience of being lowered down a shaft. "There were two gormless men gabbling and chattering at t'winch on top, and they let him go too sudden. Parker brok beath legs." A ganger's length was between two and three miles and at Blea Moor Old Tom Mason's length took in the tunnel and perhaps fifty yards on either side. He contrived to work outdoors in good weather and under cover when the weather took a turn for the worse.

In the old steam days, smoke from passing trains—especially double-headed trains—could reduce visibility to zero. "Blea Moor was a terrible place," said a member of the Tunnel Gang, who was paid half a crown a week extra for working in Blea Moor. He was lucky. Harry Cox, who worked in the Tunnel prior to 1914, said there was no extra pay. The company did allow each man a white blanket coat. "I ask you—white!" A man was also provided with thigh-length leggings. "Naptha lamps were used. If a man felt a little devilish, he'd 'accidentally' knock one over. Then the tunnel seemed to be on fire.''

A man who worked in Blea Moor during the 1930s said: ''It used to upset a lot of people. The smoke hung about for days on end. We had Tilley lamps and then they got around to having electric lights at the tunnel side. I'd see little bulbs burning here and there, if the visibility was reasonably clear. In winter I used to go into t'tunnel when it was dark and come out after it was dark. I wondered what I was doing with my life!'' The life-expectancy of a rail in the sulphur-ridden tunnel was about ten years—half that of a rail which had been laid in the open. ''The place stunk o' sulphur. Once they had us painting the rails to mak 'em last longer. You either heard dripping water—or nowt, till a train was coming. Then you'd dash for cover in one of them little manhole places cut into t'tunnel side.''

Norman Dobson remembered when, in the Thirties, it was decided to re-lay the track in Blea Moor Tunnel. Gang 201, which would be involved, was only at about half its usual strength. ''It was Sunday work. The company thought it was uneconomical to run a ballast train from Carlisle as well as one from Hellifield, so the Carlisle and Appleby men travelled by express train to Settle on Saturday night and roughed it in cabins. I decided to travel down by motor bike. I left home in good time, at about 4 a.m. It was cold and wet. Before I got to Musgrave, there was sleet in the air. At Kirkby Stephen, heavy snow was falling. The snow in Mallerstang had frozen and the road was like glass...In Blea Moor, we were at least away from snow and ice. The re-laying went on apace. And when it was over, the members of Gang 201 were given a lift to Blea Moor box.''

When, during the 1939-45 war, news reached Dent station of some deaths in Blea Moor Tunnel, Cecil Sanderson stopped the first train and boarded it with some stretchers from the Home Guard stock which was kept in the waiting room. The accident happened at about 4 a.m. News of it took a little time to reach Dent. Sandy recalls: ''We took three stretchers and put them on the brake van. I asked the driver of the train to stop when he had entered Blea Moor Tunnel and I would get off.''

Before Sandy and the driver entered the tunnel, he had a word with the ganger, Charlie Campbell, and a group of men, including his lengthmen, who were in the cabin at the north end of the tunnel. ''I explained that I had the stretchers and needed someone to give me a hand. When we had accounted for the men we would send for the Sedbergh ambulance. The fellows were devastated. Some of them had been in the gang coming through. There was one volunteer. (It was later revealed that both his father and grandfather had been killed in accidents in that very tunnel).

''We had only paraffin hand lamps at that time. I said to the engine driver that I would walk in front of his engine and would keep the lamp behind me so that he might see where he was. After a few yards, the evidence of a terrible accident was smeared on a sidewall and bodies were in what from a distance looked just like heaps of clothing. We had no idea who these men were. It was revealed that they were the special tunnel gang which operated from the Ribblehead side of the tunnel.

''They had entered the tunnel to do some work at the north end. They were walking on the up-line, facing the traffic, which was all right, when they heard the sound of a train coming in from the north end, facing them. Instead of finding the first available recess in the tunnel wall, a recess put there for safety reasons, they stepped across on to the down-line on which the parcel train (bearing newspapers and items of post) was running; they had their backs to it. The noise of the train approaching them drowned the sound of the parcel train, which usually had only two coaches on it and was the fastest train on the Settle-Carlisle. It ploughed into this gang of men.''

Sandy had to deal with matters concerning an express train

derailed in Rise Hill Tunnel. A broken driving rod had dug into the ground, bending outwards. As the train was coming through the tunnel, the rod dug into the side wall. A derailment followed.

In the summer of 1958, the author had the rare chance of walking through Blea Moor Tunnel. The Settle-Carlisle was still thunderous with steam trains, and it was consoling to have the company of the tunnel inspection group. Outside, there was an overall greyness from the sky, and grey mist clung to the hollows. One shade darker than the mist were jay-walking sheep. So it was a relief to get undercover. Men who had been working in Blea Moor since a much earlier hour were enjoying cups of tea. Standing on the up-line were a box-type wagon, with a special framework on top, and an ordinary wagon containing wedges, cement, sand and brick.

Mr A Gardner, chief works inspector, clambered on to the roof of the main wagon with an inspector and three men who carried small hammers and spears on long rods. Another inspector sat in the other wagon, holding a sheet of paper on which to record observations on the state of the tunnel. At a signal from Mr Gardner, seven railwaymen put their shoulders to the wagons and sent them rumbling towards the tunnel mouth. I walked with Mr J E Turner, engineering assistant in the office of the District Engineer at Lancaster.

The tunnel has a crown, haunches and sidewalls. Tablets on the sidewalls give the distance from the tunnel mouth, counting from the southern end. Any part of the masonry might have its position clearly delineated. Men with hammers tapped like amorous woodpeckers with the object of finding any brickwork which was "drummy" or hollow. Any "spalling" or soft masonry would be knocked down or it would fall on to passing trains. The spearmen probed into the joints. Their spears were made from worn-out shovels. I heard the rumble of the wagons, the hiss of paraffin lamps and the chanting of the railwaymen as they reported on the state of the brickwork. "Hold it, lads," came a muffled shout and some soft masonry was brought down, the position being noted so that the wound might be healed. Mr Turner examined the sidewalls. He rubbed his finger on the masonry, showing me the mixture of soot, mud and water. One of the men remarked: "Thee wait till we get diesels. Then we'll be white-washing the tunnel."

From far up the tunnel came three blasts on a whistle. Someone yelled: "Train on the down." I felt compression on my ear drums. There was a shriek from a locomotive. The sound reverberated through the huge cavern. "Clear the six foot," came another anonymous voice. This was in case a wagon sheet on the approaching goods train was flapping. A man would be hurt badly if the train was travelling at between fifty and sixty miles an hour. Another train whistle; then the locomotive thundered past, a few yards from where we were standing. Firelight stained the darkness. I heard a staccato clattering of wagons. Then—silence. Smoke billowed down from the head of the tunnel, blotting out the friendly circle of daylight which was the tunnel mouth.

At this point, five hundred feet below ground level, the first impression created by the passing train was of size. In the open air, trains are often dwarfed by the landscape, but this moaning monster filled half the width and almost the height of the tunnel. It was the only train to pass through during my tour. The smoke was by no means as thick as it might have been. Members of the tunnel gang have told me of visibility being almost down to zero and of having to walk along, their guide being a stick tapped against one of the rails. One of the men advised me to slip the bottoms of my trousers into my socks. "Then you won't have smoke pouring from under your collar!"

We progressed in fits and starts, with the men on the roof of the wagon intoning like high priests at a subterranean religious ceremony. We passed under Shaft No. 3, which is 390 feet deep. It was ten feet in diameter. I saw the brickwork and the "garlands" which catch water and direct it into a downspout, which in turn empties into the main drains of the tunnel. What seemed to be a spider's web at the head of the shaft was the grill preventing foreign bodies from falling on to the tracks. No. 2 shaft, at 358 feet, was equally impressive. Wisps of smoke hung about in the void. And then we had reached No. 1 shaft, at 217 feet. The tunnel itself was featureless, apart from the recesses into which railwaymen go when trains are approaching. There is also said to be a "donkey hole"—and a small seam of coal. As I left the inspection party, who were about to return on the up-line, one of the men said: "Tha's bin lucky today. Tha'll nobbut need a wesh when tha gets home. Most days we need a bath—and change t'watter several times an' all."

THE HOT END OF THE FOOTPLATE

Social Life

There was a library at the station. Nobody seemed interested. It just went. We used to have church services in the waiting room on the "down" platform. There was a little harmonium, and sometimes we'd have a dozen worshippers. Dances were held in the Tank House. That's all gone... When the wind blows at Garsdale today, there's not a lot to stop it.

An old-time railwayman, 1984.

IN THE 1930s, Garsdale—at the other end of the Coal Road from Dent—was a thriving community. The station even boasted of a library, the nucleus of which had been given by a local lady. The Stationmaster acted as Librarian. Dances were held in the Tank House, the walls of which were flanked by seats taken from an old carriage which, divested of its wheels, was brought to rest beside the Tank House to act as a supper room, where dance patrons could buy cups of tea and sandwiches. "It was the recognised thing among t'older lads to take their lady friends through into t'old railway coach for supper.

"Those dances were what you might call Sixpenny Hops. There was quite a lot of space, enough for fifty people perhaps. Two big coal-burning stoves kept the place warm. There was always a dive for the few available seats." When Mr Cobb was stationmaster, he played the accordion for dancing. Sometimes a piano was in use. Up to fifty people could dance at a time and the floor was "one of the best floors you could wish for."

Sandy and his wife attended some of the local "do's" but he was fond of more reflective pastimes. His love of fishing has already been mentioned. One of his favourite haunts was

WATER TANK AND COMMUNITY CENTRE, GARSDALE

Hell's Cauldron, where the River Dee tumbles into a deep pool, with some of the water flowing from it on the surface and some taking a subterranean course between beds of limestone. A feature was the Devil's Pulpit, a natural piece of sculpture, shaped by the swirling water over many centuries. "I used to sit in the Pulpit and look into the pool. Now and again I saw an enormous fish. It may have been a salmon-trout. It seemed to spend part of his life in the underwater cavern. When it did show itself, I fancied that it responded when I called to it—'Jet—come back; come back; come on...' It seemed to half turn over and look up. Then it would quietly swim back out of sight."

The War Years

ON THE day war broke out (as the comedian Rob Wilton said at the beginning of one of his famous monologues), Cecil Sanderson, the Stationmaster at Dent, and his wife, Florence Margaret, were holidaymaking in the Lake District, more precisely Lakeside, where lived a great friend who in summer was in charge of the steamboat service. "We arrived on this particular Sunday morning and when we walked into that house, we were invited into the lounge. The wireless was on, with an announcement that war had just been declared. There had been rumours of war, and Chamberlain had been waving his cards about, but we just could not believe it had happened..."

Even in 1939, before war had been declared, there was much military material on the railway. Railwaymen were aware of an impending crisis. The driver of a freight train heading for Carlisle saw a troop train moving south. "Everybody was saying there was going to be an invasion." A Hellifield driver who signed on before noon had told his wife to expect him home shortly after 8 p.m. "I was due out of Carlisle at six-something." It was wartime, but he had been told that traffic had eased a little. At Long Preston box, the fireman went to sign in for him. He asked the signalman about the situation ahead. "There was a train standing at every box to Carlisle."

In 1939, the railway was in good order, much of the line having been re-layed. All the stations were blacked out. A handlamp was placed at the end of each platform to help drivers. "If you couldn't see, you could hear. You were accustomed to the sounds of viaducts and cuttings and over-bridges." The trains now clattering through Dent were

TRANSPORTING TANKS BY RAIL

longer and heavier than ever. Piloting was in the luxury class. Bigger locomotives were called for and bridges were strengthened to take them. Two "Jubilees" which had been re-built with larger boilers made their appearance on the Drag in 1942. A year later, rebuilt "Scots", of the 4-6-0 arrangement, made their Settle-Carlisle debut and, without aid, could be persuaded to take a train of almost any length. Six of these locomotives, stabled at Holbeck, Leeds, hauled almost all the expresses until well after war's end.

So Dent station went to war. The radio played lively tunes, such as Eric Coates's melody which was adapted for a long-running series, *Workers' Playtime,* and recorded voices sang *Run, Rabbit, Run* and of the day when we'd be Hanging Out the Washing on the Siegfried Line, Vera Lynn sentimentally foretold of a happy end to the war as, to moistening eyes, she mentioned Bluebirds crossing the White Cliffs of Dover. A guard on a goods train which was rattling along the fell-edge track near Dent on a sunny morning was smoking a cigarette and admiring the trough-like valley far below when a Spitfire fighter aircraft appeared and flew alongside the train. The pilot and the railway guard waved at each other.

Events to raise money for the Red Cross were held at Dent School and the *George and Dragon;* at Cowgill School and at the Garsdale Tank House. Sandy and his wife were among those who trudged over the Coal Road to Garsdale to attend a whist and dominoes drive in the unique setting of a room under a huge tank which supplied the station and thirsty locomotives with water. "Mind you," says Sandy, "it wasn't winter-time."

Sandy's wartime staff at Dent consisted of Violet Sutton and Bill Chapman, who were both classified as porter-signalmen. The women of the Settle-Carlisle wore "civvies". Only the men had uniforms. Bill, a quick but neat writer, was especially useful when a sheep sale took place in the upper dale. By the time the animals had been driven up the hill, Bill had all the necessary documents prepared. Rowland Sanderson, who had a depot at the station, was never known to complain. "He'd do anything, would that lad."

Black-out curtains fitted to the signal box came to within a foot of the floor. The windows were covered with cellophane glued to the glass. The lamp permitted at night shone merely on the train register. The box had an in-built air raid shelter— and a tin hat was available for the signalman.

All the staff at Dent station were included in the local unit of the Local Defence Volunteers (LDV or "Look, Duck and Vanish"). The force was re-named Home Guard. "We were trained on the firing range at Sedbergh School. It was here we had talks about the dangers of 'careless talk' which 'costs lives'. We had to be careful about anything we said about the railway and to whom. The signalmen were instructed to keep the box door locked. Each night, there would be five or six men, with a specified number of hours on duty, patrolling the line from Rise Hill down to Blea Moor tunnel, and off-duty men relaxing in the ladies waiting room, which Sandy had converted for military use. "We had stretchers in there for weary men to lie on." The Home Guard based on Ribble-head patrolled up to the Blea Moor signal box.

Dent Home Guard did not go through a pitchfork stage. Up at the Station, Sandy decided to set up a firing range at Dent station. The firing would taKe place between two rows of snow-sleepers, and the marksmen would be firing uphill. Any stray shots would end up in the sleepers. "Instead of having ordinary Lee Enfield rifles, we had .22 rifles, borrowed from people in Dentdale." South of Blea Moor, the Home Guard had the task of guarding Ribblehead viaduct. Each evening, a Service rifle was loaded in case the Germans decided to parachute into the area. And each evening, in the waiting room of the station, was enacted the routine of accounting for the ammunition. Once, a cocky member of the Force said he had already removed the ammunition. To prove it, he pulled the trigger of the rifle. There was the Grandfather of Big Bangs. A bullet sped through the ceiling, then the slates of Ribblehead station and (happily) headed in the right direction—outer space.

One winter night, when because of heavy snow there had been single-line working at Dent for about a week, a large number of trains loaded with tanks, guns and ammunition were to pass through Dent, en route for Scotland. "They were heavy trains. The gradient, the curviture and the weather were against them. We were informed of this by Skipton Control, who said we must keep the trains moving as close together as was possible, though we must not try to do anything clever with them. I advised the signalmen down to Settle and said: 'For God's sake, don't let me down. We mustn't have any fiddling about with these trains because Control have told me that the Chief Operating Manager is on his way up from Derby to clear the line at Dent'."

Sandy could not believe that someone as high up the ladder as the Derby official would concern himself with a matter which was already being dealt with adequately at local level. Sandy received a phone call when the Chief reached Leeds and said: "I want to get up there straight away. Stop all the traffic and let me get through." Sandy replied that if this happened, the conditions were such that the trains—ammunition trains for the war effort—would never get restarted. The Man from Derby said he knew that, but they must be kept out of his way. He insisted on this, with all the authority of his office.

CLEARING A PATH THROUGH SNOW

Sandy put the receiver down knowing the revised scheme would not work. He had spent a week on single-line working, in appalling conditions, and here was someone coming up from Derby to tell him what it was like. The Chief Operating Manager began clearing a path for himself by giving instructions to the inspectors and signalmen on route. He asserted: "If you have a train coming, shunt it! And let me get up there!" Sandy was at Garsdale when a message reached him that the Manager had arrived at Dent Head. He took the ploughs on the single down-line (the up-line was blocked between Rise Hill and Dent Head) and had a word with the signalman at Dent, who gravely informed him that the Chief had reached Dent Head and wanted to see Sandy, who suspected that Dent might be requiring a new Stationmaster.

The Chief Operating Manager sat in his saloon. There was just a locomotive and the saloon. Sandy walked to it from Dent Head signal box and was soon face to face with his boss. "Sanderson—that is your name?" Sandy steeled himself for a rebuff. Instead, the Chief said: I'm very sorry. I had no idea what the conditions were like. But I'll get that line cleared out tonight." Sandy doubted if this would be possible and said: "When the moon gets up tonight, a strong wind will blow from the north-east. It's been like that every night." The Chief said: "I have two hundred troops coming from Carlisle. And I can get another two hundred from Leeds. I'll get that line cleared." Sandy said he did not think this was possible, whereupon his boss wagered ten shillings he could do it.

Asked what time he would be back on duty, Sandy said: "Six o' clock in the morning." The Chief was sure that by this time, the line would be clear. Sandy was out of bed just before 6 a.m. He rang Bill Bannister, the signalman at Dent Head, asking brightly: "Is the line clear, Bill?" He replied: "Is it heck!" Nothing had been done. The troops arrived from Carlisle and went to where the line was blocked. The snow-ploughs hit the Garsdale water-troughs and came "off the road" (losing the vital element in the battle against the drifts and blocking the up-line, thus making the situation worse than it had been). The troops had just nicely arrived at the site when an officer told them to get back into the train and prepare to return to Carlisle. The conditions were not fit for man nor beast. They had left by 1 a.m.

The Chief Operating Manager, who had been sleeping in his saloon, eventually arrived at Dent, told one of his men to give Sandy a ten shilling note and said: "I just cannot believe there's weather like this. I just cannot understand it..." Sandy, hearing about the withdrawal of the Army before they had done anything, took the opportunity to praise the lengthmen, who worked in such grim conditions week after week, without grumbling or complaining, though they had not got the equipment or special clothing, footwear or food available to the Army.

Just after war broke out, Mr Braithwaite, ex-Lord Mayor of Leeds, bought Whernside Manor. Wagon loads of material—furniture and fittings—arrived at Dent station. The material was transported from the station yard to the Manor by the dependable Rowland Sanderson, and at the end of the month the Stationmaster went there to have the railway account settled and to receive payment for the delivery charges. "Mr Braithwaite used to invite me into the house for a chat." Rumours circulated that he was generating his own supply of electricity, using the power of a beck flowing from Whernside.

At night, the dalesfolk lay in their beds and listened to aircraft droning overhead. "You could tell which were the Germans. You got to know the sound of them." The Observer Corps had a look-out post beside the Coal Road, a few hundred yards up from Dent Station House; it was their task to record and report enemy activity in the air. It was supposed that the Germans were anxious to locate the Settle-Carlisle because of its wartime role in handling traffic—men, munitions, even tanks—to and from Scotland. "Germans used to come over most nights, droning over the top of my house. They would drop flares and incendiaries, sometimes an odd bomb, though you would not hear much of it because the sound was deadened by peat."

The Home Guard were called out following a report of a parachutist seen descending over Widdale Fell. Sandy says: "This was in broad daylight. The report came from Jack Akrigg, the ganger at Dent, who kept the Cow Dub pub, now known as *The Sportsman's Inn*. John (Jonty) Parkinson, one of his lengthmen, a witty man with a fund of amusing stories, had not left work at Dent station. He immediately got his motor bike. I grabbed my rifle. (The wardrobe at the Station House was full of guns and ammunition). I gave Jonty a rifle. We set off, scoured the Widdale area but never found anybody." Focal points on the line appear to be have been used by aircraft heading for Manchester, Liverpool and Barrow-in-Furness. Two bombs fell at Hollow Mill Pasture, just across the railway from the box, and one night the Rise Hill side of the valley was sprinkled with incendiary bombs.

Trains conveying tanks to Warcop for training were a familiar sight. "We used to go down to Kirkby Stephen and we picked up conductors to take us on to Warcop and Clifton Moor. I collected one conductor—he was a driver on the railway and also a bookie. He said: 'Will you be on this job tomorrow?' I said: 'I can't really tell.' It varied a lot. A lot depended on when the specials were running. I asked him why he was interested. He told me he wanted to go hound-trailing somewhere in the Lake District and he could do with a lift to Appleby."

The line carried a lot of specials, including troop trains, prisoner of war trains, ambulance trains and iron ore trains. A Hellifield driver recalls going out to relieve the driver of a prisoner-of-war train which was going south. "In charge of that train were American troops. They got out on the plat-form at Hellifield and stood there with their tommy-guns." Another time, he was told to relieve the 10-25 train from Leeds to Glasgow. He found a soldier on the footplate and there was a gun at the back of the tender. "He must have been expecting something."

Sandy recalls being on the up-line platform as a trainload of troops from Scotland arrived. The platelayers had been clearing the platform edge of snow so that passengers could stand well clear of the train in case someone swung open a door. One of the soldiers asked where he was. Somone men-tioned Smolensk, a Russian town which had been on the news that morning.

Then there was the misty early morning, half way through the war when there was a bustle at the Stationmaster's House as Sandy and his wife prepared to go off for the day. Floss (as he called his wife, after her first name, Florence) shouted downstairs: "There's someone at the front door." Sandy, in the process of shaving, had his face lathered-up as he opened the door. "There was this blood-stained man standing there. I thought he must be a motor-cyclist and asked him if he had been in an accident. He said: 'Yes—I have.' He staggered back. 'Are you all right?' 'No—I'm not but I'm not as bad as the others'.''

He related, haltingly, that a Lancaster bomber with a Canadian crew had crashed on the felltop. He, the rear-gunner, had managed to break his way out of the turret. The pilot, co-pilot and front gunner were dead. The navigator was in a terrible state. Sandy went to the bottom of the hill and told Mr Middleton, a shop-keeper who also had a taxi. His wife contacted Sedbergh police, who in turn reported the crash to the RAF. Sandy then accompanied the rear-gunner up the Coal Road, where they met the dazed and bemused navigator. He asked: ''Where are we?'' And Sandy said: ''Near Dentdale.'' ''Where's that?'' ''Between Widdale Fell and Whernside.''

He was taken to the Stationmaster's house, where Floss served cups of tea and something to eat. Sandy deduced that the aircraft had been operating from Leeming. It had been flown to the French coast on a bombing mission, which had been successful. The crew were on their way back to Leeming when the accident occurred. Sandy brought out a map and pointed to Leeming and Dent. The navigator was distraught at the thought of being so far off line.

Afterwards, Sandy was told that when low cloud formed it had been decided to dive to get below the cloud. They struck the top of Widdale Fell. The aircraft shot along the ground, hit a wall and flipped over on its back. The aircraft came to a standstill in a peat bog. The survivors had heard the sound of trains—these were the armament trains on the Settle-Carlisle line—and when dawn broke the two active members of the crew made towards the sound of the trains. Their route was straight down the Coal Road to Dent station—and the home of the Sandersons. ''They were very nice men. We had letters from them afterwards.''

Sandy occasionally walked down to the *Sportsman's Inn*, formerly The Cow Dub, which was owned by Jack Akrigg, one of his gangers. Jack also had a smallholding. Sandy would go to a door at the side of the building, lift the latch and step into the pub to hear Jack shout: "Come in, Mr Sanderson." On a winter night when Sandy's visit to the Sportsman's was partly for the walk, to get his blood circulating in a cold snap, he said to Jack: "What puzzles me is—how do you known it's me when I walk through the door? And before I speak?" Jack said: "It's t'way you lift the latch."

The war ground on. No one seemed to be singing about the Siegfried Line after the shock of the Evacuation of Dunkirk, though Vera Lynn's Bluebirds were still waiting to cross Dover's White Cliffs. At Dent, there was an occasional sprinkling of incendiary bombs. The Young Farmers' Club had a social as well as an educational round and was also, unofficially, a matrimonial agency. Down in the dale, fields which had not been touched, apart from muck-spreading, for donkey's years, were now being turned "brown side up" for the war effort. Land Army girls were to be seen.

The Sandersons' table at Dent station was sometimes distinguished by red grouse, disturbed from the moor by shooters and brought down by Sandy, who used drystone walls, or even one of the snow-fences as butts. There were "black game" in the area. In winter, with his son, Sandy would climb The Fell (Great Knoutberry), seeking out the head of a gill where blackcock could be seen in an area where thorn bushes provided them with berries.

A local farmer, Mr Mason, encouraged him to shoot rabbits and said he would supply him with as much ammunition as he required for this purpose. "I used to get the cartridges at a shop in Kirkby Stephen. I'd take the train to Kirkby Stephen and put a bike in the guards van. Instead of returning home by train, when I'd done the shopping and had a haircut, I'd cycle back through Mallerstang, over by Aisgill, down Garsdale and back home via Sedbergh. By the time I'd climbed the Coal Road to the station, I was ready for my tea!"

Several men had farming connections. For them, food rationing was no hardship. On a farm there was allus a bit o' summat extra. A tale went the rounds of a Lunesdale farmer who was good at rounding up surplus pork and lamb and selling it without wanting to see anybody's ration books. He set off one day with his wife, using t'owd van, and they were returning with a good load when they were waved down by an inquisitive policeman. The farmer kept his foot on the throttle and shot by the startled constable. His wife is reported to have said: "Now you're for it—he'll sewerly have got thi registration number." The farmer said: "Doan't worry lass. Just afore I set off from home, I smeared t'number plates wi' cow muck."

Just before another wartime Christmas, Sandy visited a railwayman who took him through to the kitchen and asked him, mysteriousy, if he would like "a bit of change"."What from?" "From nowt." The man went to the oven and brought out a huge ham. Said he: "Have a slice or two of this." Two or three large slices were duly cut and wrapped up so that Sandy might take them home to his wife.

Another evening, the man asked his opinion about a large painting he had bought, saying: "Do you think it's beautiful." Sandy replied: "It's rather good." He could not honestly say it was beautiful. His host asked him if he would like to see it working, which seemed a strange comment with regard to a painting. "So he got hold of the picture and lifted it down. Behind it were two little doors. He opened them and I saw two shelves, laden with pig meat—sides of bacon and hams. He'd secreted them away in a little cupboard he'd made, using some of the chimney space."

More blatant was the notice which the signalman at Langwathby was said to have put on the door of his box: "Rabbits and Eggs". A train stopped half a mile down the track and back-backed. Said the driver to the signalman: "Can I have a couple of rabbits, Andy?" The signalman said: "Aye, grand—five bob a couple." The driver said he'd like some more. He'd be coming this way again on the following Wednesday.

Andy's son, when on duty at Kirkby Stephen, was asked by the Leeds driver of an express which stopped unofficially: "We're getting terribly short o' food in Leeds. Any chance of getting any eggs?" The signalman replied: "I'll get you as many as you can cope with." The driver said he was on such-and-such an express in the following week and "I'll stop and pick 'em up. Don't worry about the delay. I'll make it right with the guard." The signalman got him eight dozen eggs. The driver was a regular customer after that. "I was going round buying eggs at 2s.3d a dozen and he was giving me 4s.6d. Apart from the 4s.6d, he was giving me an extra ten bob for missen!"

Just before the Second Front (the Invasion of Europe) took place, a trainload of jeeps went by. Americans were sitting in the jeeps. It was so cold, they had kept the jeep engines running. And the headlamps were blazing. "The drivers of other trains just couldn't reckon it up." When war ended, the Settle-Carlisle had been thrashed almost to death by the demands made upon it. Winning the peace was to prove another most difficult operation.

Brave New World

We are seeing the Dales die and we want to do all we
can to keep them alive. The railway does more than give
us a way out—it gives other people a way in.
George Ellison, chairman of Dent Parish Council, 1968.

I look to all who have promised to support the line to
work together to ensure that it has a successful future so
that the case for closure does not re-emerge.
*Paul Channon, Transport Secretary, refusing consent to
close the line, 1989.*

DENT station not only survives but looks smart,
with its privatised buildings well-maintained and the
station as a whole having a tidy, well-cared-for
appearance. Also on the credit side are the lengthening of the
platforms and the replacement fencing in the familiar
diagonal pattern of the old Midland days. Early in 1995, work
began on the re-roofing of the up-platform waiting room,
which normally has an array of helpful leaflets—and
sometimes the odd vase of flowers.

In winter, an old blackcock perches on the thorn tree across
the tracks, with the hard northern light giving its dark
plumage some silvery highlights. I have the fanciful idea that
the blackcock, a bird of the open ''white'' country, is looking
glumly towards Dodderham Moss which, with the lusty
growth of massed conifers, now resembles an outlier of the
Canadian Backwoods. Spring speckles the lineside with
diminitive blooms. In summer, the heather which thrives on
dry bankings, fenced off from hungry sheep, displays its tiny
purple blooms. The rosebay willow herb is clad in imperial

purple before the seeds, light as thistledown, are wafted far and wide by passing trains.

On the debit side, the signal box has gone. Dent was one of the "small" stations and therefore any lost structure is a major loss. Settle-Carlisle enthusiasts wince when they see the patch of flat ground where it once stood. It is pleasant to recall the cheerful face of Jack Sedgwick peering from behind the broad windows. I sometimes call to see Jack's widow, who lives at Dent Town, and we talk our way back down the changeful but basically happy years.

Sprinters maintain a weekday service which whisks local people to the fleshpots of Carlisle, Settle, Skipton or Leeds. Hundreds of train-spotters and photographers gather on days when Steam Specials storm the Drag. Are they still known a grykers, a reference (somewhat obscure) to the enthusiasts who volunteered to clean an engine which would shortly be used on the Settle-Carlisle? It is said that they cleaned that half of the locomotive which would be visible to them. The rest remained mucky! Train-spotting breaks down the barriers of class, creed and wealth. A well-grown man takes on the mental age of eleven. The spotters carry expensive cameras and tape-recorders. They no longer swear when a long sunny spell is followed (at train time) by the arrival of cloud, with the prospect of rain—which is typical Settle-Carlisle weather.

A plume of smoke appears to view as far down as Blea Moor. Enthusiasts watch, with mounting excitement, as the train crosses the viaducts and runs along the ledge to Dent. On a calm day, those assembled on the bridge smile as their lungs take in the old familiar sooty tang, but on most days the smoke does not hang about. The Pennine breeze disperses it over hundreds of acres of soggy landscape.

Ninety trains a day went through Dent station. Towards the end the locomotives looked careworn, with dirty faces—a scratch collection of motive power filling in the gap before the ultimate triumph of Diesel. The footplate men were characters all. They had their own lively way of talking about their jobs. Bill Addy told me of absorbing the fantastic heat from the fire on one side while, eight feet away, there was ice on a bucket. Bill had fired engines while wearing his heavy mack. "The rain was coming down so heavy, it was washing the muck down. It didn't wash the cobs down—always the muck and slurry, and you were throwing that on your fire. On some engines, such as Crabs, the fire doors have a handle to open and shut them. You'd have your driver standing there and as you came round with the shovel, he'd open the doors. You'd sling in whatever you'd managed to pick up. As soon as you pulled t'shovel out, he'd shut them again. He didn't want both cold air *and* rain to get in!"

By 1936, motor traffic was affecting what had been a lucrative freight business. Passenger takings at Dent were £35 to £50 per month. Most of those who travelled were wives and widows of railmen using free tickets for market day travel from Dent or Garsdale to Settle or Hawes. When the Hawes pick-up was stopped, Dent was closed to goods traffic. It was supervised by the Garsdale Stationmaster. And that was that—until the Settle-Carlisle got the equivalent of the Kiss of Life.

But first there were the heartbreak years. The Hawes branch closed in 1959 and the track was lifted. Dr Beeching included the line in his rationalisation proposals of the 1960s. Closure was avoided but some intermediate stations were lost. By the early 1970s, mid-day trains had ceased to run. The Thames-Forth express, subsequently known as the *Waverley,* vanished from the timetable when the Waverley route was closed down in January, 1969. The Thames-Clyde was stripped of the title which had given it an aura of romance and now the train stopped only at Skipton, Hellifield, Settle and Appleby. In its northward journey from St Pancras, it was somewhat slower than its predecessors had been sixty years before. The Settle-Carlisle lost the patronage of St Pancras, where I used to stand, amid the milling crowd of London commuters, listening with barely-concealed joy as the station announcer ran through the litany of Settle-Carlisle stations, including Dent.

Nottingham was now the starting point for the anonymous Settle-Carlisle expresses. When local services were withdrawn on May 5, 1970, only Settle and Appleby remained. The line which British Rail seemed intent on phasing out, through re-routing traffic along the East Coast route and not pumping money into the maintenance of non-vital structures, did come back into its own when there was diversionary traffic, as when the Lancaster-Carlisle was closed on Sundays for engineering work. Up at Dent, the fiery dragons re-appeared high above the dale as well-lit but diesel-hauled trains sped across the skyline.

Working Steam vanished from the Settle-Carlisle for ten years, then returned in a glamorous new form, the Steam Special, packed with enthusiasts. Thousands more lined the trackside to gape or photograph the *Green Arrow,* as she sped northwards in mist and wind-blown sleet. Driver Cyril Patrickson, of Skipton, one of the cheerful volunteers who took hold of the controls of steam locomotives (and rejoiced to have the help of an especially large footplate staff) recalled for me the pleasure of taking the *Flying Scotsman* over the line. Patrick's father was proud of the honour which had come to his son but then said of this famous locomotive: "It's a blooming Geordie." The wife of one driver who had been thinking of volunteering for Steam Special duties told him to forget it. As she explained to a neighbour: "He's had a mucky job for years. Now at least he comes home from his diesels clean and tidy. And he's going to stay that way..."

Dalesrail, an imaginative scheme devised through co-operation between British Rail and the Dales National Park, was inaugurated in 1975 and led to DMUs stopping at various stations, including Dent. Dalesfolk could now go shopping at big centres, such as Carlisle and Leeds, and townsfolk might explore wide tracts of upper Dales country without having to worry about where to park their cars. Among the popular walks on *Dalesrail* days were those from Garsdale to Kirkby Stephen stations. Walkers might go via Wild Boar Fell or Mallerstang Edge. During its most popular phase, *Dalesrail* catered for over 500 people on a single day.

LOGO FOR THE CENTENARY CELEBRATIONS

The romance of Steam was enjoyed early in 1980 with the running of the first of many Cumbrian Mountain Expresses. The 1980s were years of anxiety. Ribblehead viaduct was reported by British Rail to have deteriorated so much it had only a few years of life left unless very expensive remedial action was taken. (In fact, having been listed as an Ancient Monument, the viaduct would have had to be maintained whether or not there was a railway operating across it). We stood helplessly by as British Rail prepared for closure of the line by stealth, not least by amending the timetable so that trains were unhandy. It is a story which has been fully told elsewhere. Into being came the Friends of the Settle-Carlisle but despite their protests, and those of many others concerned about the railway, the objectionable changes to the timetable were found to be absorbed when it was issued in May, 1982. The Settle-Carlisle passenger service was debased. The freight service was switched to other tracks. And, peevishly, someone decided that the Settle-Carlisle would no longer be used for diversionary purposes.

The next bright idea was to snip the Settle-Carlisle into two sections, that in the north stopping at Appleby and that in the south having its termination at Ribblehead quarry. The result would be two mineral lines. And in December, 1983, a formal closure notice was published—on the very day a severe derailment on the West Coast main line led to the diversion of traffic over the Settle-Carlisle. The campaign waged to keep the line open—and to disprove many of the figures being quoted by British Rail—have been well documented.

A bright spot came in the summer of 1986 with a subsidy provided by local authorities to run a regular *Dalesman* service of two trains each way between Skipton and Carlisle. Some of the existing Leeds-Carlisle trains made extra stops. A mini-bus service connected Sedbergh and Hawes with Garsdale station. In the following year, the service was further improved. Privatisation was mentioned, and bids invited, against an impressive increase in the number of passengers carried by the Settle-Carlisle as the result of an improved service. There was political juggling. Could anything save the line?

Unexpectedly, on April 11, 1989, the situation was transformed when Paul Channon, the new Transport Minister, rose to announce what most people expected him to say—that after consideration, the Settle-Carlisle would be closed. Instead, he refused British Rail consent to close the line. It took everyone by surprise. Factors involved in his decision included the increased revenue and a sizeable reduction in the estimated cost of restoring Ribblehead viaduct. The Minister hoped the private sector, in conjunction with British Rail, would be involved in developing the route. He backed the establishment of a trust fund to help pay for the

Ribblehead repairs. Thus ended a gruelling and protracted campaign by the Friends, Transport 2000 and the Railway Development Society, supported by local authority and well-wishers among the ranks of the political parties. During the eight years of uncertainty, a vast number of ordinary folk—not forgetting a dog, the pawprint of which appeared on a petition—had supported the campaign to keep the Settle-Carlisle open. Peter Horton, chairman of the Joint Action Committee, remarked: "This is a great triumph for the hundreds of thousands of people, from the length and breadth of this country, who have campaigned for this result. We pay tribute to each and every one of them; for their efforts, their individual sacrifices and, most of all, to those who are no longer with us."

The Settle-Carlisle has survived. Up the Drag, through the tunnels, over the viaducts, and through tiny Dent station, come the trains—Sprinters, long and lean like greyhounds, a regular freight train carrying ash from the power station at Drax to an industrial project at Kirkby Thore, plus Steam Specials. At Dent, the deep cuttings which once occupied many of the energies of the Slip and Drainage gang are now relatively stable, but a shiver passed along the line at the end of January, 1995, when a particularly wet spell of weather caused landslips to occur, one of them above Mallerstang. On an evening when the wind howled and water streamed down as though from a celestial hosepipe, a Sprinter was de-railed and slewed across both tracks.

What a journalist called a "black hole" in communications meant that the driver could not use his cab-radio link to inform Control at Carlisle. The message went via Settle and was promptly dealt with, but by the time it reached the box at Kirkby Stephen where an up-train was due, the train had already gone by. For several minutes it sped through the stormy darkness of one of the remotest stretches of the line. For Control and the signalmen those six minutes before it collided with the de-railed train were the longest six minutes of their lives.

On my latest visit to Dent station, it was dull, dry but very cold. The westering wind had an edge to it like Sheffield steel. At the Stationmaster's House, where Jenny talked about the family association with the highest mainline station, I asked her what it was like to live there when the wind was strong. She replied: "Cold. You have to put three thousand jumpers on. It makes you wonder why you're living here. Humans shouldn't be here, really. Natural elements come into their own."

We were wind-assisted in our walk along the platform beside the up-line. Here and there the wind played a tuba solo with some obstruction. Our walk took us close to the old goods dock. We sheltered in the lee of the station buildings, now a private house. When Roy and Jenny Holmes first knew Dent station, in the 1970s, the main building was rented out to a school from Burnley. It was while helping the school with some practical jobs that they first became interested in the Stationmaster's House. "We thought it would be lovely to

come and live up here. We managed to scrape up enough money to buy it."

They bought the house in 1977, a year after the Settle-Carlisle centenary was celebrated, and it became their residence in 1981. The weather became a dominant force in their lives, though at that time conditions were neither as wet or windy as they are today. "We had long, cold spells which brought snow. Sometimes we had difficulty in getting up the hill. Once we were stopped by a thick layer of ice." Another time, a gale took the chimney off the house and lifted the carport, dumping it in the beck. Jenny showed me some of the drawings she had made in the early 1980s, when "oh—it was a lovely station".

Jenny has sometimes had to play the role of rescuer. Two boys who were trudging over Newby Head in grim weather ran the risk of suffering from hypothermia. "They were walking the Dales Way in the middle of winter. I picked them up and brought them up to Dent station, where we dried them out. We get Christmas cards every year from them...Two other boys, having walked over Ingleborough and Whernside, decided to go home. They came up to the station to inquire about the time of the next train. This was November. At that time there was a very limited service. We had to tell them the next train would arrive in—April. They asked about the next bus and we said: 'Saturday—from Sedbergh'. We just accept, when living here, that we have to help people. We just can't turn people away."

Tackling the Snowdrifts

Sandy recalls two adventures in snow.

We had an exceptionally bad snowstorm. The cutting outside Dent Station House, where I lived, must be about 50ft high and yet it was half-full of snow. An express train ran into it! The first rule on the Settle-Carlisle when snow was sticking was that the ploughs should be sent straight up to Dent. Control relied on local knowledge. I was the only stationmaster on the Settle-Carlisle line who had a telephone at his bedside, for use when I was on call.

When the express ran into trouble, we had been ploughing the up-line out with the snowploughs. The storm was so bad that in a few minutes, or so it seemed, it had filled in again. Now we ploughed out as far as we dare go to the engine. Then it was up to the platelayers to use their shovels. They must clear as much as they could while the wind was slack. It would soon blow up again.

We made a tunnel up the side of the engine to the footplate, where we found the driver and the fireman were almost exhausted. We got them out and took them down to the cabin near Dent signal box. It was a lovely warm cabin, for we were never without coal up there. There was so much traffic in those days, and particularly in wartime, that if a signalman was getting short of coal the driver (if he had a goods train, which was travelling slowly) would slide a couple of shovelfuls of coal over the side at the signal box.

We brought the starved footplatemen round with the Dent cure—OXO and Bovril, and food provided by Skipton or Hellifield when the storms occurred. Sending provisions was a regular thing. Cheese sandwiches were the mainstay.

Another time I went to clear a snowdrift at Dent Head viaduct. The line between Dent and Ribblehead was the only stretch which needed clearing and the big drift lay between here and the north portal of Blea Moor tunnel. It was deep and I thought—if I'm going to clear that, I'll have to get some speed up.

There were two engines, back to back. When we went over Dent Head viaduct, I thought—we're off the road! The footplate shook violently. The fireman was jumping up and down. We hit this snowdrift—and went straight through it. Everything went dark. We were in the tunnel and could settle down again. Then I noticed that the fireman was covered with snow. One of the look-out glasses was broken. At the drift, the snow had squeezed through and looked like a ruddy sausage.

Vital Statistics

The Settle-Carlisle extends from Settle Junction to Petteril Bridge, a distance of rather more than 72 miles. About two-thirds of the line are in the county of Cumbria.

The 1 in 100 gradient is attained immediately and continues with little remission for 15 miles to Blea Moor Tunnel, where the highest point is 1,151 ft. Beyond the tunnel, the gradient eases a little.

The summit of the line (1,169 feet) is attained near the site of Ais Gill signal box.

Blea Moor Tunnel, which has a length of 2,629 yards, was cut (in the period between 1870 and 1875) through gritstone, shale and limestone. The Tunnel Gang used to talk of the thin veil of coal they had found. The Tunnel has a maximum depth below the moortop of 500 feet.

Rise Hill or Black Moss Tunnel lies to the east of a line originally chosen by the surveyors. It was driven through blue limestone for 1,213 yds. Work on the two shafts was begun in May, 1870, and the miners who worked south from Shaft 2 met others working north from Shaft 1 on March 21, 1873. The complete breakthrough occurred in 1874. The deepest of the shafts is 147 feet.

Dent Head Viaduct, which stands at an elevation of 1,150 feet, and spans the nursery reach of the River Dee, was constructed of blue limestone (the celebrated Dent Marble) and consists of 10 arches, having a length of 199 yards and a maximum height of 100 feet.

Arten Gill Viaduct, which to me is the finest of them all structurally, is not as originally planned. An Act of Parliament in 1871 granted a deviation or the structure would have had a height of 167 feet. The Viaduct consists of 11 arches which, unusually, were turned in stone, not brick. Dent Marble was the material used, the work of construction began on May 3, 1871 and the task was completed by April, 1875. The Viaduct has a maximum height of 117 ft and a length of 220 yards.